D1830747

ARCHAEOLOGY
IN
INDIA

WORKS BY THE SAME AUTHOR.

ILLUSTRATIONS OF THE ROCK-CUT TEMPLES OF INDIA. 18 Plates in Tinted Lithography, folio; with an 8vo volume of Texts, Plans, &c. 2*l.* 7*s.* 6*d.* London, Weale, 1845.

PICTURESQUE ILLUSTRATIONS OF ANCIENT ARCHITECTURE IN HINDOSTAN. 24 Plates in Coloured Lithography, with Plans, Woodcuts, and Explanatory Text, &c. 4*l.* 4*s.* London, Hogarth, 1847.

THE PALACES OF NINEVEH AND PERSEPOLIS RESTORED: An Essay on Ancient Assyrian and Persian Architecture. 8vo. 16*s.* London, Murray, 1851.

THE ILLUSTRATED HANDBOOK OF ARCHITECTURE. Being a Concise and Popular Account of the Different Styles prevailing in all Ages and in all Countries. With 850 Illustrations. 8vo. 26*s.* London, Murray, 1855.

HISTORY OF ARCHITECTURE IN ALL COUNTRIES FROM THE EARLIEST TIMES TO THE PRESENT DAY. In Four Volumes, 8vo, viz.:—

HISTORY OF ANCIENT AND MEDIÆVAL ARCHITECTURE. Two Vols. 63*s.* Second Edition. London, Murray, 1874.

HISTORY OF INDIAN AND EASTERN ARCHITECTURE. One Vol. New Edition. 42*s.* 1876.

HISTORY OF THE MODERN STYLES OF ARCHITECTURE. One Vol. 31*s.* 6*d.* 1874.

TREE AND SERPENT WORSHIP, OR ILLUSTRATIONS OF MYTHOLOGY AND ART IN INDIA, in the 1st and 4th Centuries after CHRIST. 100 Plates and 31 Woodcuts. 4to. London, India Office; and W. H. Allen & Co. 2nd Edition, 1873.

AN ESSAY ON THE ANCIENT TOPOGRAPHY OF JERUSALEM; with Restored Plans of the Temple, and with Plans, Sections, and Details of the Church built by Constantine the Great over the Holy Sepulchre, now known as the Mosque of Omar. 16*s.* Weale, 1487.

THE TEMPLES OF THE JEWS AND THE OTHER BUILDINGS IN THE HARAM AREA AT JERUSALEM. London, Murray, 1878.

THE PARTHENON; An Essay on the Origin and Construction of Greek and Roman Temples, with especial reference to mode in which Light was introduced into their interiors. London, Murray, 1883.

ARCHÆOLOGY IN INDIA,

WITH

ESPECIAL REFERENCE TO THE WORKS

OF

BABU RAJENDRALALA MITRA.

BY

JAMES FERGUSSON, C.I.E.,

F.R.S., D.C.L., LL.D., V.-P. R.A.S., &c.

LONDON:

TRUBNER AND CO., LUDGATE HILL.

1884.

ARCHAEOLOGY
IN
INDIA

BY

JAMES FERGUSSON, C.I.E.,

F.R.S., D.O.L., LL.D. V.P. R.A.S., & C.

GYAN

Published by

Gyan Publishing House
5, Ansari Road
Daryaganj, New Delhi-110002
Phone: 011-47034999, 9811692060
E-mail: books@gyanbooks.com

Distribution Network
gyanbooks.com
India, USA, Canada, UK, Australia, France

© Publisher

All rights reserved. No part of this work may be reproduced, stored, adapted, or transmitted in any form or by any means, electronic, mechanical, photocopying, micro-filming, recording or otherwise, or translated in any language, without the prior written permission of the copyright owner and the publisher.

ISBN : 978-81-212-4494-7 (HB)
First Published, 1884

2nd Impression 2020

Printed at: Gyan Press, Delhi.

The book is sold subject to the condition that it shall not, by way of trade or otherwise, be lent, resold, hired out, or otherwise circulated without the prior publisher's written consent.

Archaeology in India
Author: James Fergusson

PREFACE.

There is a French proverb that says, "Qui s'excuse s'accuse;" and there is an English free translation of the same to the effect, that a man who pleads his own cause, before an authorised tribunal or before the public, has a fool for his client. There is much worldly wisdom in each of these sayings, and, no doubt, in nine cases out of ten, where a man has a grievance and feels sure of the justice of his case, he had better leave it to others to vindicate his rights. Sooner or later, the discrimination of the public and their sense of justice will set the matter in its true light, and do for the aggrieved party what he can never so well do for himself.

Yet there is no rule, however so general, that has no exceptions; and the present appears to be so exceptional a case that an author can scarcely refrain from noticing it, though in doing so he may lay himself open to the imputation of egotism. In the first place, the personal question is of so infinitesimally small importance to the general public, that no one would probably take the trouble of noticing it except the author, while it is so involved that no one, who has not followed it from the beginning, can possibly state it clearly. In the second place, it is so insignificant, that even I would be content to pass it over in the silence I have maintained for the last ten years, were it not that Babu Rajendralala's[1]

[1] Throughout the following pages I have felt considerable difficulty in knowing how to designate the hero of the story. His full style and title is Babu Rajendralala Mitra, C.I.E., LL.D. Rai Bahadoor, which is of course too long for repetition. C.I.E. carries no honorific designation. LL.D. is merely an honorary degree of the Calcutta University, and no more makes him a doctor than an Oxford or Edinburgh honorary degree entitles me to call

attacks on me are enshrined in the magnificently illustrated volumes issued by the Bengal Government, which naturally invest them with an exceptional importance they otherwise would not possess.

Of course I do not for one moment mean to insinuate that the Bengal Government intentionally employed Babu Rajendra to misrepresent me or to depreciate my works, but, either through ignorance or indifference, they did allow him to use their resources to an unlimited extent for that purpose. Having, for motives to be explained hereafter, chosen to pick a quarrel with me, the Babu availed himself of the opportunities afforded by the reports he wrote of his mission to Orissa [1] in 1868–69, and to Buddha Gaya,[2] 1877, to such an extent that these works have become practically gigantic pamphlets written for the purpose of exposing my iniquities and ignorance. Had he done this in his private capacity, I should not have felt called on to notice the criticism of one who knows so little of the subject, or is actuated by such motives. When, however, the matter has the *imprimatur* of a Government like that of Bengal, it assumes at the present day an importance in the eyes of the public, it would not otherwise have: and may, hereafter, lead future inquirers into errors on this subject to an extent it will be difficult for them to detect when all the actors in this absurd drama have passed off the stage.

---

myself Dr. Fergusson, which I certainly *am not*, while Rai Bahadoor is untranslatable. In the following pages I therefore propose calling him by the name by which he obtained his name and fame as a Sanscrit scholar, and by which he is easily recognised. The title Dr. Mitra, by which he is now sometimes called, is new and unfamiliar. I propose, therefore, in the following pages to style him by his old familiar name of Babu Rajendralala Mitra, or, where no ambiguity exists, it will be convenient for shortness to call him only "The Babu" *par excellence*. There is no disrespect meant by this. It is merely done to avoid unnecessary prolixity.

[1] 'Antiquities of Orissa.' By Rajendralala Mitra, LL.D., C.I.E. Published under the orders of the Government of India. Two vols. folio. Calcutta, 1876, 1880.

[2] 'Buddha Gaya. The hermitage of Sakya Muni.' By Rajendralala Mitra, LL.D., C.I.E. Published under the orders of the Government of Bengal. Calcutta, 1878.

I am of course aware how thoroughly thankless and unprofitable a task I have undertaken in writing and publishing such a work as this. As the editor of the 'Academy' said some time ago: "Into the controversy with Mr. Fergusson about the origin of Indian Architecture we do not propose to enter. There is hardly a third man living who would care to mediate between the two"[1] (Rajendra and myself).

The unfortunate part of the business is, that the editor is probably quite correct in his description of the state of affairs. There are not, so far as I know, probably a dozen of persons in this country—nor, I am sorry to think, even in India—who care two straws about the origin of Indian Architecture; and I, at least, do not know one who would take an interest in the present question, except, of course, a personal friend who might feel interest in what concerns me individually.

Under these circumstances it may appear the height of folly to publish on such a subject; and, were I guided by the ordinary motives that induce men to rush into print, I should refrain. But in the present case it appears to be a sufficient excuse that *I* take an intense interest in the matter, whatever other people may do, and can afford to indulge in my whims. The public can easily protect themselves by refraining from buying or reading my book, if they feel no interest in the subject, which will not break my heart.

If it were only to protest against the misrepresentation of my writings and their meaning by Babu Rajendralala, it certainly would not be worth my while to undertake it. These can do me no harm, and may safely be left to the oblivion they deserve. But I am desirous, before leaving a subject with which I have been so long connected, to obtain an opportunity of saying a few last words on some points of Indian archæology which recent experience have rendered clearer to me than they were before, and the Babu's works are a convenient peg to hang my observations on, which otherwise would require lengthy dissertations to make their application obvious.

I am anxious also, before it is too late, to raise my voice against the practical destruction of ancient Indian monuments,

[1] 'Academy,' April 1882, No. 518.

which has lately been going on. Under the specious plea of restoration, many of the most important of them have been subjected to a treatment by which some of their most interesting features have been entirely obliterated.

Beyond these motives, also, this little volume will enable me to recapitulate some of the results of my latest investigations in Indian archæology. It is a growing and rapidly progressive science, continually yielding results tending to modify conclusions previously arrived at, and offering new developments of the utmost interest to those who can appreciate their significance. The principal elements of the problem were ascertained by me during my travels in India between 1835 and 1842, and I have since seen no reason to unsay anything I said on the subject when I first published my work on the 'Rock Cut Temples' in 1845. But half a century's experience since I first took up the study has induced me to modify some of the details, of which I did not at first see the significance, and has enabled me to write with greater precision and with more confidence on many matters than I could at the earlier period, and I gladly avail myself of this opportunity of recording this improved knowledge.

The real interest, however, of the volume—if any—will probably be found to reside, not in the analysis of the archæological works of Babu Rajendralala Mitra, but, in these days of discussions on Ilbert Bills, in the question as to whether the natives of India are to be treated as equal to Europeans in all respects. Under present circumstances it cannot fail to interest many to dissect the writings of one of the most prominent members of the native community, that we may lay bare and understand his motives and modes of action, and thus ascertain how far Europeans were justified in refusing to submit to the jurisdiction of natives in criminal actions.

Left to themselves, the natives of India possess many virtues and many noble qualities, which render them worthy of the esteem and admiration of all who have had familiar intercourse with them; but these have rarely, if ever, been enhanced or improved by contact with European civilisation. Wherever our influence extends, we have destroyed, or at least weakened, the influence of caste which, though, in itself, hardly conducive to virtue, simulates morals so perfectly as to become indispensable for the regulation of Indian society. In its place we have tried to introduce the loose regulations of a form of civilisation the natives can neither understand nor appreciate. Instead of the religion, which governs every action of their life, we have tried to substitute an education, which they cannot assimilate, and which in consequence remains, in almost all instances, a useless and empty platitude.

So little do we understand the nature of the people we have undertaken to govern, that we petted and pampered the Sepoys till they thought they were our equals, and that we were afraid of them. Being an army more numerous as ten to one, they believed themselves equal to the task, and as patriots felt called upon to deliver their country from the dominion of strangers, and the result was the Mutiny. The present sentimental attempt to place "Young Bengal" on an equality with ourselves, may not have so prompt and decisive an answer, but it must lead to one more fatal to our moral influence, and probably more disastrous to the good government of the country.

If this is so, it is easy to understand why Europeans resident in the country, and knowing the character of the people among whom they are living, should have shrunk instinctively, with purely patriotic motives, from the fatuity of the Ilbert Bill. It may, however, be useful to those who reside at a distance, and who have no local experience, to have it explained to them by a striking living example, wherein the strength and weakness of the cause resides, and for that purpose I do not know any example that can be more appropriate than that of Babu Rajendralala Mitra. If, after reading the following pages, any European feels that he would like to be subjected to his jurisdiction, in criminal cases, he must have a courage possessed by few; or if he thinks he could depend on his knowledge, or impartiality, to do him justice, as he could on one of his own countrymen, he must be strangely constituted in mind, body, and estate.

CONTENTS.

LIST OF WOODCUTS.

CHAPTER I.

INTRODUCTION.

PERSONAL.

Although the study of Indian Archæology may to most people appear a very insignificant and trivial affair, to me it happens to have been far otherwise. Though I will not say it has been the most important business of my life, it certainly has been its most important recreation, and I have derived from it more enjoyment than from perhaps any other source. I began the study some fifty years ago, at the time when the genius of Prinsep was re-creating, and breathing fresh life into the chaotic mass of idle fables, which, before his time, represented the history and doctrines of Buddhism. The chronology of the sect and the biography of its founder were then daily assuming shape and becoming clearer; but little had been done to ascertain what their architecture had been, or to discriminate what really belonged respectively to Buddhism, to the Jains or to the Hindus, still less had the origin of these various forms been traced, or how they arose, and what their influence was on each other. What little had been attempted, was of the haziest and most tentative character.

Seeing and regretting this state of things, I determined, as far as in me lay, to try to remedy it, and the success that attended my endeavours to effect this rendered the next few years perhaps the happiest of my life. Even now I look back with more pleasure to the time I spent in this investigation than to any other epoch in my life. Nothing could exceed the delight I experienced in visiting the various cities of Hindostan, so picturesque in their decay, or so beautiful in their modern garb. It would be difficult to realise any greater enjoyment than wandering with my small sowaree of well-bred camels among the wildly picturesque scenery of Rajputana, and visiting all those scenes and cities over which the writings of Tod have shed such a halo of romance. But beautiful though the scenery of Central India may be, and romantic as its history certainly is, the interest of Western India, to an archæologist, is centred in its caves. Situated in picturesque glens or in solitary rocky places, all the religions of India have left imperishable records of their religious aspirations in these localities, such as must interest every one capable of sympathy with the devotional feelings of his fellow-men.

Day by day, as I wandered through these beautiful regions, the conditions of the problem I was attempting to solve became more and more apparent. Nowhere are the styles of architecture so various as in India, and nowhere are the changes so rapid, or follow laws of so fixed a nature. It is consequently easy to separate the various styles into well-defined groups, with easily recognised peculiarities, and to trace sequences of development in themselves quite certain, which, when a date can be affixed to one of the series, render the entire chronology certain and intelligible.

Before I left India the styles were all perfectly well defined in my mind, the sequences determined and the dates at least approximately fixed. Since then, by collecting photographs and following up the information that has since been obtained from inscriptions and other sources, I now feel sufficient confidence to boast that if any one would produce me a set of photographs of any ancient building in India, I would tell him within fifty miles of where it was situated, and within fifty years of when it was built. He would be a bolder and more confident man than I am who could feel sure that this may not be proved to be wrong hereafter, but up to the present time I see no practical difficulty about it,—within certain limits of course.

The extremely favourable circumstances under which I entered upon so engrossing and fascinating a pursuit, the study of Indian Archæology became sufficient to render a ten years' sojourn in India singularly enjoyable. But in addition to this, all my relations with the natives of India were of the most gratifying and satisfactory nature. From the Rajahs of Central India, who afforded me princely hospitality, and assistance during my various journeys, down to the native servants who remained with me from first to last during my sojourn in India, all my intercourse with the inhabitants of the country were of the most agreeable nature. I was proud to enumerate among my personal friends many of the upper classes in Bengal, and all my relations with them were pleasing and cordial; while I shall never meet again with a set of servants who served me so faithfully, so honestly, from the time when I first landed in India till I left its shores. I never had a dispute with any native of the country, nor harboured any angry feeling against any one, and when I finally left the country, every recollection of it and its inhabitants was of the most pleasurable nature. I left India with regret, and should willingly have returned to scenes of so much enjoyment, if circumstances over which I had no control had not prevented my so doing. The first unpleasantness that has occurred to me during my connection with the country and its inhabitants, has been this gratuitous and most unexpected attack on me and my works by Babu Rajendralala, and which has given rise to the present protest, against the terms in which it is formulated.

When I left India the Mutiny had not occurred to disturb the relations between Europeans and natives, and more than this, the party usually designated as "Young Bengal," did not then exist. These are the creation of another age and another state of things, and are one of the most unsatisfactory results of our attempts to force our civilization on a people not yet prepared to receive it. One of the first effects of educating any set of men beyond anything known in their own class, and of treating them as equals before they have acquired any title, morally and intellectually, to be considered as such, is to inspire them with the most inordinate conceit in themselves. They soon learn to consider themselves not as equal to their former masters, but as superior, and they turn round and glory in their own fancied superiority. Nothing could exceed the "furore" with which the whole native press of Bengal, a few years ago, exulted in abusing every member of the European community. No character, however respectable or respected, was safe against its attacks. Facts were of no consequence. It was so much easier to invent than to collect them, that they could be supplied to any extent on any given occasion. The thing at last became an intolerable nuisance, and it was to try and stop this that the Vernacular Press Act of 1878 was passed unanimously by Lord Lytton's Council. It might have been wiser to despise it, and leave it alone to cure itself; but gross unfounded slander and misrepresentation are hard to bear, and those who are unfamiliar with the extent to which it was carried on are hardly fair judges of the feelings which led to its enactment. The outburst can only be compared to the delight with which an emancipated slave turns to abuse his former master when he feels he can do so with perfect immunity from any evil consequences to himself; and of this, under our sentimental government, he easily could feel so assured.

The Act has since been repealed, in whole or in part, and I have no means of knowing how far its action tended to repress the public expression of the slanderous attacks against which it was directed. But the feeling remains, and it may consequently be interesting to present to the public a portrait of one of the best and most typical of the class. If it is well drawn and a good likeness, politicians, even in this country, will be able to understand why Europeans in India object to be governed by Bengalis, and why all this agitation has arisen about what to them appears an infinitesimal grievance. Though Indian Archæology may be considered as beneath the attention of the English public, the Ilbert Bill is certainly not so, and no means of bringing it home, and rendering it intelligible to the masses, appears to me so appropriate as examining a typical specimen of one of the proposed class of governors, and seeing what stuff they are made of. For this purpose there is probably no example so suitable as Babu Rajendralala. He has written in English more, and under more favourable circumstances, than any native of Bengal, and has consequently, laid his aspirations his mode of attaining them more bare than any of his *confreres*, so that out of his own mouth it will be easy to judge how far the class to which he belongs are worthy of the confidence it is proposed to repose in them.

No one who has resided long in Bengal, or has been in familiar intercourse with the educated classes of the natives of that country, but must have been struck with the marvellous facility with which they acquire our language, and at least a superficial familiarity with the principal features of our arts and sciences. The truth of the matter is, their powers of memory are prodigious. No other nation in the world could have handed down their earliest literature from primæval times to the present day without the intervention of any kind of writing. But it seems an established fact, that till nearly the Christian era, the Vedas were transmitted from generation to generation by oral recitation only, and that even now Brahmins can be found who can commit the whole to memory, and repeat it consecutively, without the aid of any written text. Memory is, in fact, the Indian's forte; but knowledge acquired by its aid only, is apt to be superficial, and sadly wanting in depth and earnestness. It is such, however, as in these days of competitive examinations would enable a native of India to distance an Anglo-Saxon easily in any struggle for pre-eminence. If a sufficient number of Bengalis could afford to come to England and reside here for the time required to prepare for their examination, the whole of the Civil Service of Bengal would fall into their hands. In the rarest possible instances could any Englishman compete with them, and if the selection were fairly made. As tested by the Civil Service examination, it would be impossible to refuse them any or every appointment, whatever we may think of their other qualifications for the Service.

Perhaps, however, the most glaring defect of this easily acquired knowledge is the inevitable conceit it engenders. A man who by his powers of memory alone has become familiar with a great mass of scientific facts, is apt to consider himself quite equal to those who, by long study and careful reasoning, have assimilated the great truths of scientific knowledge. Without any previous study or preparation, he does not see why he should not "profess" any science he may take a fancy to, and pronounce dogmatically on any series of facts that may come before him.

On any other hypothesis it is difficult to understand how a scholar like Babu Rajendralala, who had fairly gained distinction by a life-devotion to Sanscrit literature, should, when long past middle age, have thought that by merely willing it, without any previous preparation, he could acquire an equal position as an archæologist.[1] In 1868, however, he undertook to conduct a party of artists and photographers to explore the antiquities of Orissa, and to bring away casts of some of its sculptures, and in 1871 to write the two ponderous tomes on the Antiquities of Orissa, which were to enlighten the world on one of the most difficult branches of Indian archæology.

To most men, if ambitious of acquiring a position among archæologists, this commission from Government would have been considered as the best possible opportunity of doing so. But to avail himself of it to any extent, certain qualifications were required of which the Babu was practically deficient. In the first place, he has no knowledge of architectural draftsmanship, surveying, or plan-drawing even to a limited degree. Besides these deficiencies, it would have required a considerable amount of hard work to examine and master the details of a sufficient number of buildings, to be able to write anything about them that would be worth reading; and a greater amount of patient study and reading to comprehend the subject fully. Neither of these were consistent with the Babu's habit of body and mind; some shorter path to eminence must be found, and its discovery does the Babu's ingenuity considerable credit, whatever may be thought of it in other respects.

[1] In the 'Journal of the Royal Asiatic Society,' in 1880, I stated very clearly my belief that, before 1871, Babu Rajendra had never turned his attention to archæological subjects. To this he replied in the 'Bombay Gazette,' May 25, that he considered these objections "very smart, not to say scurrilous," which may be considered by his countrymen as a sufficient answer to me. But to a European it would have been more satisfactory if he had referred to some work or paragraph in any work he had written, showing that he had, before 1871, turned his attention to the subject. As none, however, are adduced by him in answer to my challenge, I presume I may consider that none such exist.

In this country the process may be said to be unknown; but in Germany—if I am rightly informed—it is not uncommon. When any professor who in his younger days has attained to eminence in any line of research, either through indolence or senility, fails to keep abreast of the knowledge of the day, some younger man seizes the opportunity to expose his shortcomings. If he succeeds, and maintains his position, he mounts on the shoulders of the superannuated professor; and from that high ground starts with a considerable advantage in the struggle for fame. If he fails, he fails ignominiously; but, in the keen competition for eminence, the risk is worth running, and the advantage of showing your superiority to a name that has hitherto been respected is so great, that it is at all events worth trying for. Some such scheme seems to have suggested itself to Babu Rajendralala, and he paid me the compliment of selecting me as the person to be operated upon.

Even then it would have required much more knowledge of the subject than the Babu possessed to enable him to point out errors in my works of sufficient magnitude to obtain a hearing from the public; but, in lieu of this, he hit on a grievance which not only enabled him, in his own eyes, to expose the errors of my ways, but to pose as a patriot before the world, and especially before his own countrymen, as defending the cause of India against the slanders of an ignorant and prejudiced foreigner!

In some of my various works on architecture, having ascertained that the Indians employed wood, and wood only, for all architectural purposes in early times, though using it with great magnificence and appropriateness, I suggested that, it was not till they came in contact with the Greeks and other nations using stone, that they thought of employing that more durable but less tractable material for architectural purposes. It certainly was so in Central Asia. The palaces of Assyria, though among the most magnificent and gorgeous which the world has ever known, are wholly of sunburnt brick and wood; not one single stone, used architecturally, is to be found in Nineveh or Babylon. It was not till Cambyses, the son of Cyrus, met with the stone-using nations in Egypt that he and his successors thought of employing it too, the stone palaces of Susa and Persepolis being the result. So it was in Lycia and elsewhere. In no instance did the Indians adopt the architectural designs of the contemporary nations; they repeated their own wooden forms in the more durable material, and we are and ought to be grateful to them for so doing, otherwise we would not know what their early architectural modes of expression really were.

A very little reflection will easily convince any one that for almost all purposes wood is a preferable material to stone or brick, especially in tropical climates, where enclosed spaces for purposes of warmth are not a desideratum. Far greater spaces can be roofed with it, with fewer points of support, and more light or air introduced everywhere. It is much more easily ornamented with carving, and it also takes colour more readily and permanently. For all palatial or domestic architectural purposes it certainly was to be preferred; so at least the Indians thought in ancient times, and so the Burmese think at the present day. So also do the Chinese, the Japanese, and in fact all the nations of the East. The one defect with which it can be reproached is want of durability, though that can hardly be laid to its charge in India, as there exists at the present day at Karli, and in other caves in that neighbourhood, woodwork that was put up in them before the Christian era, or 2000 years ago. Notwithstanding this exceptional durability of teak wood, my impression is that the White Ants had much more to do with the adoption of stone as an architectural material than any æsthetic or constructive consideration, or certainly than any mania for copying from the Greeks or any other nation. As far as splendour or beauty of design are concerned, it is much to be regretted that they ever abandoned their first favourite material. We, however, have benefited thereby, but only because, before they did so, they left in the rock, copies of the wooden buildings they had been accustomed to erect in, or near their cities, and so preserved to our time a knowledge of the early forms of them, which otherwise would have been lost to us in consequence of their not using the more permanent material.

Having in the course of my investigations ascertained that the Indians used wood, and wood only, in all their architectural works up to the time of Asoka (say 250 B.C.), it occurred to me that the case was so nearly parallel to that of Persia, that I ventured to suggest that they had taken a hint from the stone-using Greeks, and adopted in their subsequent works the more durable material. At the time I attached very little importance to the suggestion, and am inclined to attach still less to it now. If any one likes to argue that the Indians, from their habit of copying their wooden buildings in the rock, acquired a fondness for the more durable material, and a familiarity with its use, which induced them to employ it in their structural buildings also, I have very little to urge against the hypothesis. It seems incapable of proof or of disproof. The change of material is of the least possible importance, as far as the Indians are concerned: it is only so to us. Had they used stone earlier, we should have been able to carry back the history of architecture in India to a much more remote period, and have been able to master many problems which are at present insoluble. But otherwise, as I have often said, one of the great charms of the study of Indian architecture is that we find a completely developed style of wooden architecture such as we have nowhere else, and can trace its conversion into lithic forms, till at last we lose all trace of its wooden origin. Though changing the material, as I said long ago, it remained throughout a "a purely indigenous art, without any trace of Egyptian or of classical art;" "nor can it be affirmed that it borrowed anything directly from Babylonia or Assyria."[1] As I have always maintained, there is nowhere in architectural history any example where we can find a style so thoroughly local and original, and where we can trace every step from the earliest "incunabula" to its decay and final absorption into other styles. Nor do I know any style that was so little influenced or so little interfered with by any foreign architectural influence.

This, however, was not the view taken of the matter by Babu Rajendra. His patriotic soul was fired with uncontrolled

[1] 'History of Indian Architecture,' p. 89.

indignation at the bare idea of his countrymen having taken a hint from foreigners, or borrowed a single idea from such a people as the Greeks, and in consequence he, after his return from conducting the Government Expedition to Katak in 1868–69, wrote in January 1871 a paper which he read to the Asiatic Society of Bengal, of which a *résumé*, written by himself, appeared in their 'Proceedings' in that month.

The motive for its appearance at that time was probably to justify the Government for having entrusted to him the conduct of the expedition to Orissa, and to prove to them how capable he was of undertaking the publication of its results, by showing his superiority to previous labourers in the field. I at least am quite unable to account for the phenomena on any other theory than this.

The following extracts will explain the nature and the line of argument chosen by the Babu:—

"An opinion is gaining ground that the ancient Aryans were not proficient in the art of building substantial edifices with stone and bricks, but that the primitive Hindus were dwellers in thatched huts and mud-houses. Mr. Fergusson, who has adopted this opinion, adds that the Hindus learnt the art of building from the Grecians, who came to India with Alexander, and that the oldest specimens of architecture in the country appear to be in the first stage of transition from wood to stone.

"It is denied" (by the Babu) "that the Buddhist religion—a mere reformation of the old Hindu faith—could have any influence in originating architecture, and the invasion of Alexander is compared with the British expeditions to Abyssinia, in which very little impression was produced on the domestic arts of the Abyssinians. It is difficult to believe that Alexander brought with him any large number of quarriers, masons, and architects, to leave some behind him for the education of the people of this country in architecture; and it would be absurd to suppose that a king like Asoka, who is presumed to have lived originally in thatched huts, would of his own accord send for architects and quarriers from Greece to build him a palace," &c.

I confess that at the time I first read this I was very much surprised that Babu Rajendra should have thought of attacking me at all, still more that he should have done so by so gross a misrepresentation of anything I had ever written. Up to that time the Babu was only known as an eminent Sanscrit scholar, of which language I knew nothing; our paths consequently had never crossed, and I had never mentioned his name nor alluded to him in anything I have ever said or written. It could not therefore be from personal feelings that he wrote. My astonishment was still greater in considering the mode of attack. I was then quite ignorant of the motives that impelled him to make it, or how he could hope to profit by it. It was not till long after that I perceived that it was only intended as a declaration of a war, which he knew—though I did not—he could carry on at his leisure under the Ægis and with the assistance of the Bengal Government.

I consequently waited for nearly two years, in hopes that the publication of the paper at length would throw some light on the subject, and perhaps solve the mystery. I then learned that its publication would probably be deferred to the Greek Kalends. In fact it never was published or intended to be. Perhaps never written, or even read to the Society; though it is very little to the credit of the Asiatic Society of Bengal that they should have allowed their principal officer, who was then, as now, practically the manager of the Society and editor of their journal, to use its pages for personal attacks of this sort, without insisting on some proof being afforded of their justice. The fact is, however, that the Bengal Society has almost ceased to concern itself with artistic or archæological matters, in which it formerly attained to such eminence, and devotes itself almost wholly to natural history, hence its members are scarcely likely to notice a matter of this sort, nor will they, unless Babu Rajendra one day decides on attempting to become as eminent in zoology as he is supposed to be in archæology.

Tired of waiting longer, I at length addressed a letter to the 'Indian Antiquary,'[1] protesting against the misrepresentations of my meaning, in the paper above referred to, and challenging

[1] Vol. ii. p. 28, for January 1873.

him to produce the passages on which he founded his accusations. Under these circumstances it appears there were—as Mr. Gladstone would say—three courses open to the Babu in his reply. First, to quote the passages he referred to; and secondly, to produce a building of an architectural character built before the time of Asoka, and so prove me to be wrong; and thirdly, to admit that he had read my works hastily and without due attention, and to apologise for having done so.

The first alternative was not open to him, because there is not a single paragraph in any work I have ever written that even by the most forced construction will bear that meaning, and the whole context shows that all I have written on this subject was meant to express exactly the contrary.

Ever since this controversy arose, both General Cunningham and the Babu have been searching all India to find some example to bear out the second contention, but hitherto in vain. At one time, indeed, the Babu gave it up. In the 'Antiquities of Orissa,' vol. 1. page 15, he says: "We do not for a moment wish to question the fact that no authentic stone building has been met with of an age anterior to the age of Asoka"—this in 1875. In 1881, when professing to reprint this essay,[1] he alters this phrase and says: "I venture to question the fact that no authentic, &c," but he quotes none nor gives any reason for his change of opinion. General Cunningham also disputes the assertion in his third volume,[2] and states: "I do not suppose that building with stone was unknown to the Indians at the time of Alexander's invasion. On the contrary, I will show in another portion of *this* report not only that stone buildings were in use before that time, but that some of these are standing at the present day." The General, however, forgot to redeem the promise so given, and though ten years have elapsed since that paragraph was written, he has not yet found time to produce the buildings he refers to. But after all

[1] 'Indo-Aryans.' By Rajendralala Mitra, LL.D., C.I.E. Two volumes, octavo. London, Ed. Stanford, Charing Cross; W. Newman and Co., Calcutta. 1881.

[2] Reports, vol. iii. p. 98, 1873.

this is merely *negative* evidence, at best, which any day may be upset by some new discovery—though it is hardly now probable—but the *positive* evidence is distinct and irrefragable. No one can look at any cave of the Mauryan era, and not see that every feature and every detail is copied from a wooden original, and that the people who used these forms did not build in stone, and had never used stone architecture in any ornamental building, though in mere "building" or engineering works, of course stone or brick was generally if not always employed.[1]

The third course I have indicated above was still open, and is the one that would probably have been adopted by an ordinary controversionalist. But if the Babu had done so, he must have admitted that he was in the wrong and so forfeited his claim to his prerogative of infallibility, and he would, moreover, also have been obliged to abandon his cause of complaint against me, and give up at once a line of argument by which he hoped to rise to greatness and fame.

It was in vain I wrote in my letter just alluded to, "My belief is, and always was, that the palaces of the Mauryan Kings of Palibothra were at least as extensive—certainly more gorgeous—and probably cost as much money as those of the Mogul Emperors of Agra and Delhi, and yet they certainly were in wood." Yet in 1878 he writes:—

[1] As I have been so voluminous a writer on architectural subjects, it hardly seems necessary that I should be called upon to define what I mean by the term, which I have always used in one sense and one only. Architecture I have always understood to apply to the *fine* art of ornamental building, either in wood or stone, or other materials, as contradistinguished from the *useful* art of building or civil engineering. I have written a good many works on architecture but none on building, and I might, I fancy, be allowed to understand the term. But the Babu has looked up his dictionary, and says, "I have always used the word architecture in the ordinary dictionary meaning of it, 'art or science of building,' and not in the æsthetic sense, of the ornamentation of buildings as distinct from the mere mechanical engineering art of piling stones or bricks for making houses" (preface to 'Indo-Aryans,' p. v). On the contrary, in all I have ever written on the subject I have made the most marked distinction between the two branches of the art of building, and as it is my works the Babu is criticising, he is bound to accept my definition of the subject; but nine-tenths of the misunderstandings and objections in his book arise from his inability to see, or unwillingness to admit, this perfectly obvious distinction.

"The admission that the Indians did employ stone in building foundations of houses and in city walls, gates, bridges, and embankments from long before Asoka's time goes a great deal farther than what its *author wished it to go.*[1] It throws on the author the onus of proving that men who could, and did, build stone walls, confined their talent to city walls and embankments, but could not, or did not, extend it to the superstructure of their houses; that having built a brick or stone foundation as high as the plinth, they encountered some obstacle, intellectual, material or artistic, to push it higher, and bring it to the level of the ceiling, until taught to surmount it by Greek adventurers or their half-caste descendants. The admission drives us to the inference, that the men who, according to Megasthenes, had built walls 30 feet high round Palibothra,[2] could not feel the advantage of having a masonry wall for their king's residence for the protection of his treasury. Such an inference is unjust to a nation whose inventive and intellectual faculties were second to those of no other race on earth, and which in the domain of philosophy attained an altitude which none has yet surpassed."[3]

He winds up with a piece of Babu English, which it is well worth quoting as indicative of the whole nature of controversy. He is evidently proud of it, as he reprints it *verbatim* in his 'Indo Aryans,' in 1881, p. 48:—

"In history, as in other concerns of the world, it is infinitely better, in any given point regarding which sufficient data are wanting, to acknowledge the fact, than to conjure up hypotheses

[1] As if any European author would argue such a question for any other purpose than for arriving at correct views on the subject, and communicating the results in as clear language as he could to his readers. The assumption of a personal motive shows that the Babu looks on it from a very different point of view. The correctness or incorrectness of any statement seems to the Babu's mind a matter of very minor importance, in comparison with the advantage supposed to be gained by showing that an adversary has made an unguarded statement, that is one that can be twisted by a forced construction into a contradiction of what he may have said elsewhere.

[2] Does Megasthenes say so? I don't know where, nor does the Babu give any intelligible reference to any such passage.

[3] 'Buddha Gaya.' By Rajendralala. Chap. iv. p. 168.

hedged in by *flimsy* pretences of 'it seems,' 'it is probable,' 'it is very likely,' which, when proceeding from men of high standing and undoubted talent, serve only to shroud the cause of truth in impermeable gloom. Ancient Indian history, from its hazy character, has suffered practically from hasty generalisations and *ex cathedrâ* assertions, and we cannot be too careful in guarding it against them."[1]

No. 1.—View of Cave at Bhaja. (From a Photograph.)

If instead of inditing sentimental nonsense about the injured feelings of his countrymen, the Babu had only spent a few hours in studying the photographs of the Mauryan Chaitya caves of Western India, such a one for instance as this at Bhaja, he

[1] 'Buddha Gaya,' chap. iv. p. 169.

could not have failed to perceive, even with his limited knowledge of art, that they were literal copies of structures, built with wood, and wood only. The sloping pillars of the nave,[1] the wooden ribs of the roof, the screen in front, the great timbers of the façade, and the ornamentation throughout, are all wooden features, and such as could not, or least would not, be used by any one familiar with constructions in stone. It is only an interior, however, like all the cave structures, both in the east and west of India, though a singularly beautiful one, and exquisitely adapted for the purposes for which it was intended. Nothing invented before or since is lighted so perfectly,[2] and the disposition of the parts, for an assembly of the faithful or the accommodation of a choir of priests, is what the Christians nearly reached in after times, but never quite equalled. Unfortunately we do not know, and probably never will, what the form of their exteriors was. But the facility with which wood could be used in framed constructions might lead them to forms of great variety and great magnificence. It is only in the seventh and eighth centuries when the Hindus took to copying these Buddhist structures in stone, that we get a hint of what their external forms were. But the Raths at Mahavellipur are undoubtedly Buddhist Viharas and Chaityas in stone, though nearly a 1000 years in date after the caves of Bhaja and Bedsa, and during that long period they have been changed and altered to such an extent as to render many features nearly unrecognisable.

[1] Among the most striking features of this and all the early Indian caves are the sloping pillars and jambs which were employed in wooden constructions to counteract the tendency to spread in these circular roofs. Even when constructed wholly of wood, this tendency is inevitable without tie-rods or tie-beams—but could be to a great extent obviated by this means. In the earlier caves as in the Lomas Rishi ('Indian Architecture,' woodcut 43), or at Bhaja, the doorway naturally follows the lines of the pillars, which both the Babu and General Cunningham persist in calling an Egyptian form, which it is not. It is one of the most certain tests of the age of the early caves that the lines of the doorways become more and more perpendicular. By the Christian era familiarity with works in stone had caused this peculiarity to disappear entirely in India, though curiously enough it was retained long afterwards in the Peshawar Valley, and in Thibet to the present day.

[2] See my work on the 'Parthenon,' p. 24.

It is easy to understand why the early Buddhists preferred wood to stone for their erections. Their worship required halls of the greatest dimension they could obtain, without vaults, which they certainly could not construct, in those early times at least. Wood was consequently the only material with which they could form watertight and ornamental roofs. The Hindus, on the contrary, in their temples only required a cella 10 or 20 feet cube, and a tower over it to give it dignity. These could be easily and better constructed in stone than in wood; theirs was, in fact, as essentially an external style of architecture, as that of the Buddhists was an internal one; hence the essential difference between them.[1] Possibly even the earliest temples of the Hindus may have been partially in wood; at least, if this were not so, it is difficult to account for their entire disappearance. We have not a trace of one anterior to, say, 500 A.D., and then the style is complete and settled in all its proportions, as if it had long been practised.

We have no means of knowing, and probably never shall know, how far this wooden architecture and the construction of these Chaitya halls extend backward. Halls larger and finer than any we now find copied in the rock probably existed at the time of Buddha's advent; but, being in wood, all of course have perished. What we do know is that in the time of Asoka (B.C. 250) at Buddha Gaya, and afterwards at Bharhut, and down, at all events, till the erection of the gateways at Sanchi, whenever they used stone ornamentally, it was as a literal copy of some wooden form, but of wood used monumentally, as it always was when employed for the display of architectural magnificence, as contradistinguished from mere constructive or agricultural purposes, which are the only ones to which the Babu's imagination seems capable of rising.

Besides this lavish amount of timber, there is every reason to believe that metal was employed to a very considerable

[1] It is curious to observe that the problem was exactly reversed in the western world about the same time. The Pagan style was an external one and the principal ornamentation of the temples was on the exterior. The early Christian churches, to mark their contempt to Pagan practices, devoted all their wealth to the interior, and neglected entirely the exterior effects.

extent to ornament and accentuate the wooden forms employed. At least, it is extremely difficult otherwise to understand many of the forms employed. The disks, for instance, on the rails, and the half-disks at the junction of the rails with the lintels, are such as might be used in metal, but could hardly have been suggested by any stone or wooden construction, and many details of ornamentation can be explained by this hypothesis which seem inexplicable on any other.

That the Chaitya halls were adorned with paintings is almost certain; there are plain spaces left apparently for that purpose, which were afterwards so employed; but paintings are perishable even in the rock, and none now remain in the earliest caves. Sculpture in stone, too, was certainly employed lavishly, not indeed in the Chaitya halls, but on their façades and in the viharas. The oldest vihara at Bhaja[1] is covered with sculptures, and so is the façade of the Ananta Cave, which is apparently the oldest cave at Katak—probably 200 B.C.; but there is no reason for supposing that even they are the oldest. The art may have been practised long before then, though probably in wood. At least, till some earlier examples in stone are discovered, this is the only safe inference.

Be all this as it may, we now know of a certainty that, during the three centuries that elapsed from the time when Asoka commenced copying in stone the wooden rails of his ancestors, till the time at least that the gateways of the Sanchi tope were finished, in the first century after Christ, the Indians had an art of architecture of their own, and practised it partly in stone, but mostly in wood, with consummate skill and beauty, and great originality. It is true, nevertheless, that the ornamental details of Asoka's Lâts and some parts of the early rails were borrowed from Assyria, or rather Persia.[2] The examples are too few for any very definite conclusions to be drawn from them; but where the constructive forms have also been copied, they go very far to prove that in the second and third centuries before Christ wood was the material used

[1] 'Cave Temples of India,' p. 513 *et seq.* pl. xcvi. xcvii. and xcviii.

[2] 'History of Indian Architecture,' woodcuts 3 to 6, and 27. Cunningham's 'Stupa Bharhut,' pls. x. and xi., &c.

for architectural purposes in Central Asia, as essentially as it was in India. The subject deserves far more attention than has hitherto been bestowed upon it; for if it can be shown that this was the case, it throws a flood of light on many details of early Indian architecture, which, without this suggestion, would remain inexplicable enigmas. They may have taken a hint as to material from the Greeks, but not one form or one detail of their architecture is to be found, at all events, till a much later period, on the Indian side of the Indus. But what is more to our present purpose is that, at that time, the upper classes of India were as far removed—probably farther—from being "dwellers in thatched huts and mud houses" as they were at any period between that time and the present day.

Notwithstanding this, Babu Rajendralala cannot shake off the idea that, unless men build stone temples and palaces, they must be savages.[1] It is this absurd contention that runs through all his reasoning on the origin and progress of Indian architecture in his ponderous tomes, and not only renders them glaring evidences of his inability to grasp the simplest archæological problems, and are as little creditable to himself as the Government under whose auspices they were published.

[1] If Babu Rajendra has a theory that the great King Asoka lived in a mud or thatched "hut" till the Greeks taught him to build a palace, or knows any one who proposes such an absurd hypothesis, he is quite right to state it, and deal with it as he pleases. It is simply absurd, however, to attempt to father such an assertion on me, without being able to adduce a single expression in any work of mine, that could by the most forced interpretation bear this meaning. It is childish to persevere in this contention after my repeated denials of any such meaning, and after my assertion that I considered the palaces of the Mauryan kings were at least as costly and as magnificent as those of the Mogul emperors.

CHAPTER II.

KATAK CAVES.

Towards the end of June 1837 I was fortunate enough to be able to pay a visit, though a hurried one, to these caves. The weather, however, was hot, and the rain heavy, as might be expected at that time of the year. The principal excavations were then inhabited by fakírs, who denied all approach to their abodes. I saw enough, however, to convince me of their extreme importance to the history of Indian art, the serious study of which was then beginning to occupy my attention.

In the following cold weather Lieut. Kittoe visited the caves; and though his visit was nearly as hurried as mine, the season of the year was more favourable, and he brought away a number of sketches. I had only time to make three or four;[1] his were afterwards published in the seventh volume of 'Prinsep's Journal' (plates xxxix. to xliv.), and, though valuable as a contribution, were very far from exhausting the subject, which I considered of vital importance to the history of Indian art. I consequently never ceased to agitate for something further being done to elucidate the matter. At last, in 1868, principally, I believe, in consequence of my lectures and my intimacy with Mr. (afterwards Sir) Henry Cole and General Scott, the Society of Arts were moved to memorialise the Indian Government on the subject, with the happy result, that it was induced to authorise the expenditure of a considerable sum to obtain casts from these caves, and other interesting archæological objects in India.

In consequence of this, in the cold weather of 1868–69,

[1] Two of these were published on the first plate of my folio work on the 'Rock-cut Temples of India,' in 1845.

a considerable party of moulders, photographers, and artists were despatched under the auspices of Sir William Grey, then the Lieut.-Governor of Bengal, to visit Katak, as I thought for the purpose of moulding and portraying these caves, and the superintendence of the whole was confided to Babu Rajendralala Mitra,[1] who accompanied it in the character of archæologist. If my hopes were high, my disappointment was equally great when I found that the party had never gone near the caves, but had spent their money and their time in taking 119 squeezes from eight different temples at Bhuvaneswara. In themselves they are pretty enough, as illustrations of Indian sculpture and ornaments, as it existed between the seventh to the eleventh century; but for any scientific purpose, as illustrating the architecture or archæology of the subject, they are absolutely worthless. I have at considerable pains arranged the set of these casts at South Kensington according to the temples to which they belong, and have tried to obtain a historical sequence; but, even then, neither I, nor, I fancy, any one else, can make anything of them. They are taken at random apparently, as they could be most easily got at by the moulders, without any discrimination and intelligible purpose.[2]

[1] I was not aware when I wrote previously on the subject that Babu Rajendra accompanied the expedition as "a volunteer without pay," and from some expressions in the official documents I inferred that he was included with the other members who clamoured loudly for an increase on their return, and which Government had so much difficulty in adjusting. As he says he was an unpaid volunteer, however, I am bound to believe him, and express my regret that inadvertently I was led into an error, for which I beg to apologise. In Mr. Locke's Report, printed in the Appendix A, it will be observed he says, "I should, however, add that it includes some expenses, which ought to be borne by the grant made to Babu Rajendralala Mitra, and which, if so debited, would reduce the item to something nearer the estimated amount." The wording is so curious, that others, as well as myself, might be misled into supposing that the Babu was a "paid servant of the Government."

[2] In a note, p. 5, of his second volume, the Babu makes merry with my mistake, in saying they spent time in "casting minarets, because there were no minarets to cast!" He forgets that I was quoting from his own official Report, reprinted in the Appendix. There "the Rajrani *minaret*, in twelve pieces, 35 feet high," is especially mentioned, and Mr. Locke in estimating the expense again enumerates this *minaret* as costing 100 rupees! What has

As they are published in the Babu's books, ii. to xx. and xxxi. to xxxvi. of the first volume, of the 'Antiquities of Orissa,' merely arranged apparently to suit the convenience of the artist or the lithographer, the confusion, that I have partially removed at South Kensington, is worse confounded; and if any archæologists can make any sequence or meaning out of them, they are cleverer than I am. There are no plans or elevations or diagrams to show whether they are architectural features, used to express or accentuate construction, or whether they are merely ornamental details to enrich the outline and to relieve barrenness of any plain part of the temple.[1]

The truth of the matter seems to be, that if the Babu, before being sent to Orissa, had ever heard or thought of the Udayagiri Caves, he had not the least idea of their archæological value. One cast in his estimation was as good as another, and he naturally preferred those that might glorify his own religion, and consequently preferred Bhuvaneswara to Udayagiri.

---

become of it I have no means of knowing. It is not among the casts sent home to South Kensington. It does not appear in any photograph I have seen, and is not mentioned in the Babu's book. I presume, however, it exists, and will turn up some day. A pillar 35 feet high is not a thing to be stowed away in a cupboard and lost sight of. It is not mentioned, so far as I can see, in the 'Antiquities of Orissa,' nor illustrated by any drawing or photograph. It is, in short, as mythical as most of the Babu's facts, and must so remain for the present at least.

[1] At p. 5, vol. ii., the Babu adds a long quotation from the late Owen Jones's 'Grammar of Ornament,' as a complete justification of his proceedings and consequent refutation of my heresies. My late friend, however, like many very clever persons, was liable to be carried away by his pen when writing on subjects of which he knew very little, and Indian architecture was one of these. If he wanted to ascertain whether "the Hindus had any fine art of architecture," or whether they were "mere heapers of stones one over the other," he could have obtained a far more complete and satisfactory answer to his question by examining a collection of photographs of Indian buildings, of which I could have lent him some thousands, than he could by any number of casts from one small group, taken unintelligently without any method or purpose.

I do not know any one who would have been more horrified than Owen Jones at the want of intelligence shown in the conduct of this expedition. If he had written these paragraphs after he knew the result, instead of before, they would, I fancy, have borne a very different complexion!

So soon as I became aware of the abortive result of the Babu's mission, I wrote out to my friend Mr. (now Sir) Edward Clive Bayley, and urged him to send another expedition to Katak, under more intelligent guidance, and offered, if the Government did not see their way to sanction the expense, to pay the cost, whatever it might be, myself. At the same time I wrote to my nephew, Frederick Fergusson, a barrister of the Supreme Court, and instructed him to pay whatever demand the Government might make on this account. No demand, however, was made. Sir George Campbell, who was then Lieutenant-Governor of Bengal, sanctioned the expenditure required, and though it was too late to do anything that year, a second expedition was sent down in 1871–72, under the direction of Mr. H. H. Locke, the Superintendent of the Government School of Design. It is to this second expedition that we owe the only correct plans[1] and the only really interesting casts, copies of which appear in the Babu's second volume. All in fact that renders his work of the smallest possible interest or importance to the student of Indian archæology is due to this second expedition.[2]

The Babu entered upon the task of historian of this great campaign with his accustomed vigour. In his second volume, page 41, he concludes a long rambling note, full of doubtful facts and mistaken inferences, with the following pithy sentence: "To persons gifted with that perfection of imagination which could, like Dean Swift, fill up a volume on a broomstick, the plasticity and elasticity of architectural and sculptural evidence may be welcome, but the stiffness of dated inscription is more agreeable to sober-minded ordinary mortals." It expresses in so few words the whole cause of quarrel between us, that he might as well have printed it on the title-page as the text on which this strange sermon of errors was going to

[1] I except of course the plan of the temple at Puri made by Radhaki Persad Mukerji, which was originally published on a larger scale and only in a reduced form in this work.

[2] These facts, with regard to the two expeditions and the part I took in urging the Government to send them, are not of course alluded to in the two folio volumes of the 'Antiquities of Orissa,' though all the circumstances of the case must have been perfectly well known to the Babu at the time.

be preached. My experience has been in almost every instance the reverse of the Babu's. It is at all times almost impossible to say, without collateral evidence, whether an inscription is integral or may have been added afterwards; and very rarely indeed does the excavator of a cave or the builder of a temple state that it was placed there to commemorate the fact. Take, for instance, the celebrated Lomas Rishi Cave at Behar, shown

No. 2.—Lomas Rishi Cave, Behar. (From a Photograph.)

in the annexed woodcut. It is covered with well and deeply cut inscriptions, which, though not dated in figures, are by the form of their characters, and from which it might with certainty be inferred that the cave belongs to the third or fourth century after Christ.[1] Yet no one who knows anything of Indian archæology can for a moment doubt that it belongs to the age of Asoka.[2] It has all the characteristics of the style we spoke of in describing the cave at Bhaja. The sloping jambs of the doorway[3] and of the principal supports of

[1] 'Journal Asiatic Soc. of Bengal, 1837,' p. 647.
[2] 'Cunningham's Reports,' vol. i. p. 47.
[3] 'Handbook of Architecture,' p. 91.

the roof, and all the wooden features of the framing, are as marked in this instance as in the other, and gradually fade out or are modified in subsequent examples. In fact the only mistakes I ever made in dating Indian buildings was when I was induced, from some cause or other, to rely on inscriptions for that purpose. To take one instance among many. When I visited Tanjore in 1842 I made up my mind, from the style, that it must belong to "the great age of the Chola dynasty, probably the tenth or eleventh century."[1] Subsequently, when Captain Tripe went there on the part of the Government to photograph it, Mr. Norman, who professed to be a competent authority, stated that it was ascertained from the inscriptions to have been built by Kaduvettiya Cholan, a king reigning in the beginning of the fourteenth century, I felt myself bound to bow to this, though it puzzled me exceedingly.[2] Since then, however, the late Mr. Burnell, the best scholar of Southern India, has really read these inscriptions, and proved that my original determination was correct. "Nearly all the inscriptions there," he says, "belong to the reign of Vira Chola, or from 1064 to 1114 A.D. Only one or two are of later date."[3] There are several, however, that are earlier, and prove that the temple was at least begun and partly built before that time.

On the other hand, from his contempt of the evidence of style for ascertaining dates, the Babu states in a note on page 24, vol. i., "One of the *oldest* and most sumptuous of its class, is the temple of Kantonuggar in Dinajepore."[4] Its date is perfectly well ascertained. It was, according to Buchanan Hamilton, built between 1704 and 1722, which does not say much for the antiquity of Bengali architecture. But no man that knew anything of the style would ever have thought it old.[5]

[1] 'Handbook of Architecture, 1855,' p. 91.

[2] 'History of Indian Architecture, 1876,' p. 345.

[3] Quoted by Major Cole in his 'Report on Buildings in the Madras Presidency, 1881,' p. 17, for an unpublished report by Dr. Burnell.

[4] There is a representation of it on p. 467, woodcut 263, of the 'History of Indian Architecture.'

[5] One day I purchased in a shop in the Strand a set of Indian photographs, but they were without any description except "Temple at Kantonuggar," and

The insolent tone of the remarks quoted above might very well be forgiven if the Babu had, when he made them, possessed a portfolio full of dated inscriptions which he was prepared to hurl at my head in refutation of my heresies. At the time, however, when he wrote it, the Babu was perfectly well aware that only *one*[1] dated inscription had up to that time been found in all India of an age at all bearing on this controversy. It is the inscription found by Mr. Burgess, in Cave No. III. at Badami, and it is dated in the 500th year from the 'coronation of the King of the Sakas.'[2] But the Babu did not dare to allude to this, but quietly passed it over 'sub silentio,' because it was evident to every one who knew anything of the matter, that Cave No. I. at Ajunta, was excavated subsequently to Cave No. III. at Badami, and the Babu's contention that its paintings—executed subsequently of course to the architecture represented phases of Indian life from 1800 to 2000 years ago,"[3] was utterly untenable.

Lately the Babu has attempted to escape from this thoroughly untenable position by insisting on what appears to have been a very venial error on the part of the late Bhau Daji. When the latter was at Ajunta, 1863, he copied a number of insignificant inscriptions on one page of his note-book and described them as inscriptions in Caves I., II., and X., without specifying which belonged to I. or II. or X. They were treated as of no importance, as they were not, and so clubbed together inadvertently either by him or his lithographers.[4]

The Babu Rajendra now insists that this proves that

Mr. Spconer could tell me nothing about them. From their style I was perfectly convinced that they must belong to northern Bengal. I consequently wrote to my friend Vesey Westmacott, then magistrate at Dinajepur, telling him of my purchase, and stating that I thought it must be in his district, and was a temple, I thought, of the beginning of the last century. He answered by return of post that it was a well-known temple, situated about 12 miles north of the station, and built at the date above quoted.

[1] The date of the Asoka inscriptions is perfectly well known, but it is from external evidence, not from the regnal dates, which are all that they contain.

[2] First Report, Belgaun and Kuladji, 1876, p. 24.

[3] 'Journal Royal Asiatic Society,' vol. xii., New Series, 1880, p. 126 *et seq.*

[4] 'Journal Bombay Branch Royal Asiatic Society,' vol. viii. p. 64.

some of these must be inscriptions in Cave No. I., though which he does not specify, nor of what value its evidence must be if it could be ascertained which it was. When I examined the cave, which I did with considerable care in 1839, I came to the conclusion that it contained no inscription. Before, however, asserting this on my own evidence, which at best could be only negative from the nature of the case, I telegraphed to Mr. Burgess, who was there on the spot to ascertain the fact. As his answer was that there is no inscription in the cave, I now assert it without hesitation, in spite of the Babu's suggestion that "it is possible that the inscriptions, which are painted ones, may have been effaced since the time Dr. Bhau Daji copied them."[1] Thus the Babu entirely ignores my unbiassed testimony, that there were none in 1839, which, to say the least of it, is a sort of impertinence no writer ought to indulge in unless he has very strong and distinct evidence to the contrary, and in this instance there is none.

Before leaving the matter of inscriptions, there is another, of no great importance of itself, but singularly illustrative of the Babu's mode of treating them.

In 1837, Captain Kittoe copied one, which was published by Jas. Prinsep in the 'Journ. Bengal As. Soc.' vol. vi., plate liv., and labelled from the Ganesa or Elephant Cave.[2] Regarding this inscription, I wrote in 1845:[3] "A combination of both methods of research (Archæology and Philology) is necessary to settle any point definitively; but inscriptions will not certainly by themselves answer the purpose, for in many instances they were cut long subsequently to the ascertained date of the cave, as in the Ganesa Gumpha at Cuttack;" and further on, page 41, "The only apparent exception is the inscription on the Ganesa Gumpha, which is in the Kutila character of the tenth century of our era; but as the cave in which it is engraved is so entirely of the same character as the rest, both in architecture

[1] 'Bombay Gazette,' May 25, 1880.

[2] There is a slight mistake in the plate, of which the Babu makes the most; instead of Elephant Cave, it ought to have been the Cave of the Elephant-headed God.

[3] 'Journal' Royal Asiatic Society, vol. viii. pp. 31, 41.

and sculpture, it cannot be assigned to a different era, and the inscription must therefore be considered as marking its conversion to the Brahminical faith." The Babu in two places professes not to have been able to find the inscription.[1] Did he look for it? Mr. Beglar was more fortunate. "A short distance from here, in the Ganeça Gumpha, so called from a sculpture of Ganeça on the wall of one of its cells," which the Babu also did not see, "there," he adds, "is the well-known inscription, near the sculpture of Ganeça, within the cave, which needs no comment from me."[2] The Babu's commentary on this inscription is characteristic. "Lieutenant Kittoe is said to have noticed a *dated* Kutila inscription of the tenth century, but I did not find it" (page 30) (neither he nor Prinsep noticed any date), "and no less an antiquarian than Mr. Fergusson has been misled by it, so as *to assign a very modern date to the Ganesa Cave on the strength of it*" (page 30).

I have since on several occasions referred to the age of this cave. In 1855, in the 'Handbook of Architecture,' on page 32; in 1867, in the 'History of Architecture,' vol. ii., page 494; in the 'History of Indian Architecture,' in 1876, and subsequently in the 'Cave Temples of India,' simultaneously with the publication of the Babu's second volume; but I have never varied in my opinion as to the antiquity of this cave. The fact is, I begin to doubt very much whether the Babu visited, some at least of the places he describes, as from personal knowledge; and I feel certain that he never read my works, except for the purpose of extracting from them paragraphs, which he could pervert to his own purpose by misquoting them, and without the context, to make it appear that I intended something I did not say, and, as he knows, never intended to say.

Since the discovery of the unique dated inscription at Badami, a dated inscription has been discovered bearing directly on the age of these caves, which ought to fill the mind of the "sober minded" Babu with delight, but I fear

[1] 'Antiquities of Orissa,' vol. ii. pp. 30, 34. Ibid. p. 10.

[2] 'Cunningham's Reports,' vol. xiii. p. 93.

will have the contrary effect, as it tells most seriously against the reputation that the Babu has hitherto been supposed to possess for knowledge of the sacred languages of the Hindus.

When Lieutenant Kittoe visited these caves in 1837, he made a copy of the celebrated inscription in the Hathi Gumpha or Elephant Cave, which had first attracted the attention of Stirling, and an imperfect copy of which was published by him in the fifteenth volume of the 'Asiatic Researches.' Though it was only an eye-sketch, the copy was so accurate, that Prinsep, with the aid of his pandits, was able to make a translation of it, which, considering the materials available, and the time it was made, was a marvel of ingenuity.[1] It left, however, some points still in doubt, which, considering the great antiquity of the document and its historical importance, it was most desirable should be removed. One of the great objects, therefore, to be obtained by Mr. Locke's second expedition was to obtain casts and impressions of this inscription, which he happily accomplished successfully, and with these improved materials the Babu undertook to furnish a revised copy of the whole inscription. In his second volume he devotes thirteen folio pages (17 to 29), to what professes to be a critical examination of it, and the result is, that he has left it more confused, and in a less satisfactory position than it was before. A better scholar than Rajendralala has now taken it up, and submitted a new translation of it to the Oriental Congress at Leyden, and Professor George Bühler has revised his text, and though he agrees on the whole with that suggested by Pandit Bhagwanlal Indraji, he suggests some ameliorations. Before attempting to appreciate the full value of this discovery, we must of course wait for its complete publication. But the most important point for our present purpose is that the translators have discovered that it is dated in "the 165th and 166th years of the Mauryan Era." The Pandit suggests that this must be taken as from the Abishek or inauguration of Asoka; but the Professor, with far more probability, that it must be taken from that of Chandragupta, which, as he states, must be either in 321 or 312 B.C.

[1] 'Journal,' Asiatic Society Bengal, vol. vi. p. 1090.

It is almost certainly the latter, as that coincides exactly with the era of the Seleucidæ—311 and 4 months B.C.—and suggests that the first Indian attempt to date from a fixed era was introduced by Megasthenes, the Ambassador of Seleucus, or by direct treaty with the King himself. But whatever the source, the date of the inscription is thus ascertained to be 146 and 147 B.C.

This, however, is very far from being the only point the Babu has missed. The king's name is not Aira, but Kharavela siri, and is dated in the 18th year from his accession in 164 B.C. In his second year he mentions a King Satakarni, lord of the western region, "rich in horses, elephants, men and chariots." Now as the Puranas, and the Nana Ghat inscription, mention a king of that name among the early Andras, the juxtaposition of the two names on this inscription promises to throw a flood of light on this hitherto obscure portion of Indian history, when correctly translated and fully illustrated, which there is now no doubt that it will be.

With the very imperfect materials at his command, and at that very early period in Pali studies, it is not surprising that Prinsep failed to make out the full import of this inscription. It is startling, however, to find forty years afterwards a man with the pretensions to learning of the Babu Rajendralala taking it up with new materials and appliances at his command, and failing so entirely to appreciate its importance or understand its meaning. Having no pretensions to a knowledge of Pali, I can personally offer no opinion on the subject, but it seems very probable that, when properly examined, the Babu's pretensions to scholarship may prove to be as shadowy and worthless as those he now puts forward to be considered as an archæologist.

I am afraid that the suggestion that the "nation whose inventive and intellectual faculties are second to those of no other race on earth" should have borrowed the idea of dating from a fixed era, may be considered as insulting, as my suggestion that it was from the Greeks that they took a hint for using stone, to supply the place of wood in the architectural parts of their erections. But whether that is considered as such or not, the exposure of the Babu's ignorance of Pali by Bhagwanlal and Dr. Bühler has certainly touched a tenderer point in his reputation than anything I ever ventured to suggest. It is unfortunate for him that there are many scholars who can judge of his linguistic shortcomings, while there are very few who can appreciate correctly the value of his blundering in the science of archæology.

The discovery of this date in this inscription, besides being most important for Indian history in many respects, has cleared away a vast deal of rubbish which obscured the early history of these caves. In the first place, it gets rid of the Babu's rather loose calculation of its age between 316 and 416 B.C.;[1] which, to say the least of it, is unsatisfactory, though comparatively unimportant. The great advantage, however, is that it sweeps away the Babu's date for the caves. At page 40 of the second volume, he says: "The principal caves may be assigned to the middle of the fourth century, from 320 to 340 B.C." Even leaving, however, the erroneous absolute date out of the question, it is, and always must remain, a curiosity of literature, how any one, even ignorant of and despising gradation of style, as the Babu does, could fancy that the Ananta and Ganesa Caves were excavated within the same twenty years! When I wrote last on the subject I made the interval 200,[2] and I am now inclined to extend it to nearly 300. The discovery of a new initial date, 146 B.C., may induce me to cut off fifty years from the earliest date, but I feel more and more inclined to add it at the other end; but absolute precision is unattainable at present in these dates. One circumstance, however, that has since occurred makes me inclined to fancy that I made the series a little too old. In

[1] When I last wrote on the subject ('Cave Temples of India,' p. 66), trusting to the Babu's scholarship, which I then was fully prepared to admit, whatever I thought of archæology, I was inclined to adopt his date, or nearly so, for the inscription, and placed it tentatively at 300–325. As the cave in which it is found is a natural cavern, wholly without architectural form or ornament, it afforded no data for the application of the science of archæology, and was of very little importance for my object. Its date therefore might very well be left to be determined by the philologists.

[2] 'Cave Temples of India,' p. 70.

his excellent catalogue of the Calcutta Museum, Dr. Anderson states (p. 6) that he has General Cunningham's authority for adopting the date I assigned to the Bharhut tope (150 B.C.), in preference to that he assigned to it in his work on the subject (250 to 200 B.C.). This being assumed, we have a series of structural buildings ornamented with carving and with ascertained dates ranging in parallel lines to these caves, and of the greatest value in approximating their dates.

The first are the Asoka rails at Buddha Gaya. It is not quite certain that they were put up by Asoka himself. They may have been added to his vihara afterwards. They certainly are not earlier, and it may therefore be assumed that their date is 250 to 200 B.C.

The next in the series is the Bharhut rails, which, as just said, date from B.C. 150, and is one of the most important documents that have added of late to our knowledge of Indian art history.

The third is the four gateways of the tope at Sanchi, which I assigned—and it has not been disputed—to the first century A.D. The earliest—the southern—having been erected in the beginning of that century; the latest—the western—towards the end of it. It may even be a little earlier.

Parallel to this we have the Ananta Cave, whose date, with our recent lights, it seems impossible to carry back much beyond 200 B.C. For the present it may be assumed to be coeval with the Hathi Gumpha, which, both from its architecture, or rather want of it, has generally been assumed to be the earliest thing there. On the other hand we have the Ganesa Gumpha, the style of whose sculptures are almost certainly identical with the style of the latest Sanchi gateways.

M. Beglar[1] describes another cave, a little lower down the

[1] 'Cunningham's Reports,' vol. xiii. p. 81. Mr. Beglar visited Katak in 1874–5, but his Report did not appear till 1882, when General Cunningham, apparently at a loss for something to publish to justify his appointment, pulled it out of his drawer, and sent it to press without taking the trouble to spend a few hours in editing it. There is a preface—of one page—which says nothing, and there is not even a footnote to say what has been done or written by Babu Rajendra and myself to bring up the information to the time of its publication. It is strange that during the fourteen years that General

hill than the Ananta, which apparently Mr. Locke did not see, and which certainly the Babu does not mention in his book. It is, however, of singular importance for our history of these caves. It is about 17 feet square, with three entrances, and the façade covered with sculptures—not figures, but architectural ornaments and emblems, which, Mr. Beglar states, are identical with those at Bharhut; and he is a competent authority on this subject. But the chief interest lies in a long inscription in the Lât character, painted on the inner wall. "The entire walls," Mr. Beglar says, "had evidently been once covered with a thin layer of fine plaster. The centre of the back wall is occupied with sculptures of the sun and moon; but on either side of the central sculpture, written on the plaster with red pigment of some kind, once extended this inscription."[1] Neither he nor the General were able to make much of it; but this painting on plaster is of singular interest, as it was so common in after times, and equally so is the identity of its sculptures with those of Bharhut.

Mr. Locke brought away two most interesting casts from the tympana over the doorways of the Ananta Cave (plates xxii. and xxiii. of the 'Antiquities of Orissa,' vol. ii.); but he stated that the pier between the outer two doors having fallen, the two other tympana were lost, and their subjects could not be ascertained. This is much to be regretted, as the two casts were of singular interest, one as representing the worship of the Tree, the other an image of the goddess Sri, both of which occur so frequently at Sanchi.[2] Of the two fallen ones, Mr. Beglar was able to ascertain that the one represented a scene in which

---

Cunningham has held the appointment of Archæological Surveyor to the Government of India he has never visited Orissa, though it is more full of objects of antiquarian interest than almost any province in his district. They generally belong to a class, however, in which he feels very little interest, and regarding which he is consequently little capable of forming an opinion which would throw much light on their history and peculiarities.

[1] As he gives no name to this cave, it will be convenient hereafter to call it "Beglar's Cave."

[2] 'Tree and Serpent Worship,' p. 105. Sacred trees are represented 76 times, the worship of Sri 10 times in these gateways.

elephants figure—probably the worship of the Rama Grama Dagoba; and, fortunately, I am able to supply in the annexed woodcut as much as remains of the other. It is of peculiar interest here, as supplying a means of comparison with the figure of Surya at Buddha Gaya, as represented by Cunningham

No. 3.—Surya in his Chariot. (From the Ananta Cave, Khandagiri.)

in vol. iii. of his Reports, pl. xxvii., and by Babu Rajendralala in the photograph, pl. L., of his 'Buddha Gaya.' On Surya's left hand is unmistakably represented the moon and stars, and on his right the world represented by a lotus flower; while in the chariot are his two wives, Prabha and Chhaya, not this time with their bows shooting at the Rakshasas of darkness, but merely accompanying their lord and master in performing his task of illuminating the world. It is also of special interest in this place as being the earliest instance of that Sun worship which played so important a part in the history of Orissa, and culminated in the great Sun temple at Konaruc.

Besides these, the Babu made a discovery which for his purpose, was much more important than any images of the sun and moon, or anything in the Hindu Pantheon. "The only carved ornament in the room" (he says) "is an image of Buddha in the centre of the back wall" (p. 32). As I had long ago made up my mind that there was no image of Buddha to be found on the Indian side of the Indus, at least, before the Christian era, or probably for a century afterwards, I was very much puzzled by the announcement of one existing in so early a cave, and took infinite pains to satisfy myself on the subject. If I recollect rightly, it was the principal subject of enquiry, in a letter I wrote to Mr. Locke in April 1878. Unfortunately, however, he showed my letter to the Babu Rajendra, and he, as the Babu wrote to his friend Mr. Arthur Grote, instructed him how to answer it. The result was that he never did so or even acknowledged the receipt! Mr. Phillips,[1] however, did visit the cave on my account, and latterly Mr. Burgess has sent me home a drawing of the pretended Buddha; so I can now speak regarding it with confidence. It is not integral; it is not an image of Buddha; it may be a Jaina figure, and may have been added to the sculptures of the cave simultaneously with the Kutila inscription the Babu found on its walls (p. 34), probably of the tenth century. It would consequently be of very little importance but for the use the Babu makes of it; but, as I had said, the caves may have "represented Buddhism without Buddha." It was indispensable, according to the Babu's system, that this should be contradicted and my ignorance exposed. The consequence is that he triumphantly refers, twice in his text and twice in the notes (pp. 32 and 33, notes 39, 41) to this figure of Buddha as a sufficient and final refutation of my theory. It is strange,

[1] 'Cave Temples of India,' p. 70.

however, that he should have chosen this example; for in 1878[1] he wrote: "If we may rely on the evidence of the great tope of Baráhut (B.C. 150), they (images of Buddha) must have come into vogue *many centuries* after the stupa;" "that tope represents scores of scenes illustrating scenes of Buddha's last as well as of his previous life, but none in which an image of the saint is being worshipped," &c.; "we look in vain for statues of the saint," and more to the same effect; yet in 1878, after various quotations from my works, sometimes garbled as usual, he adds: "The Buddha in the Ananta Cave is, I believe, enough to explode the theory of Buddhism without Buddha as regards the caves under notice." The truth of the matter is, the Babu knew as well as I did that the figure in the Ananta Cave did not represent Buddha at all; but the temptation of contradicting me, proved so irresistible that the correctness of the allegation seems to have been of comparatively little consequence in his eyes.

I suspect that when the matter comes to be carefully investigated, it will be found that the Indians borrowed from the Greeks some things far more important than stone architecture or chronological eras. It is nearly certain that the Indians were not idolaters before they first came in contact with the Western nations. The Vedas make no mention of images, nor do the laws of Manu, nor, so far as I can learn, any of the ancient scriptures of the Hindus. Buddhism is absolutely free from any taint of idolatry till after the Christian era. So far as we can at present see, it was in the Buddhist monasteries of the Gandara country, where the influence of the Græco-Bactrian art is so manifestly displayed, that the disease broke out, which was afterwards so completely to transform and pervade the outward forms, at least, of all the ancient religions throughout India.

Another proof which the Babu adduces to prove the Buddhism of these caves is almost too ludicrous to require refutation. In the first bas-relief in the Rani-ka-Núr, two animals, said to be young elephants, are represented to the left, in a cave among some rocky ground. It is a scene very like that

[1] 'Buddha Gaya,' p. 128.

represented in plate xxix. fig. 1, of my 'Tree and Serpent Worship.' In the Katak example, however, the rocks are more conventional, but it certainly requires a vivid imagination to convert a rocky landscape into a Swastica! even supposing that to be necessarily a Buddhist emblem; but unless there were Buddhists in early Italy and in earlier Asia Minor, the theory will not hold water. Certainly, in this instance, a rocky landscape—though I cannot compliment the artist on his mode of representing nature—is not, however, sufficient to prove the Buddhism of the caves.[1]

There is only one other point that I need refer to here, as I have sufficiently expressed my opinions with regard to these caves in another place.[2] At page 10, vol. ii., the Babu reproaches the architect of the Ganesa Cave with having made "a *stupid blunder*" in the setting out of the façades, and he refers to it again on page 45. To my mind this "stupid blunder" shows such an advance in the art of design that it is one of the principal reasons why I consider the Ganesa Cave subsequent to the Rani-ka-Núr. In the earliest caves, such as the Ananta, the sculpture was confined to the tympana of the doorways. Later the whole of the spaces between the doorways were sculptured, but, except from the interruption caused by the heads of the doorways, there is no proper separation between the bas-reliefs, though they certainly do not form one continuous subject, and most probably were meant to tell quite different stories. At least, so it appears to me in Rani-ka-Núr. In the Ganesa Cave there are four doorways, and consequently five spaces. The architect in consequence adorned the two half spaces at the ends, and the centre one, with merely architectural details, and reserved the two remaining spaces for two figure subjects, which no doubt in this instance were meant to treat of quite different subjects. One was a replica of the second scene in the Rani-ka-Núr, but in a more advanced style of sculpture. The other, which is full of action, has no affinity with any scenes represented in that or in any other

[1] 'Antiquities of Orissa,' vol ii., p. 8. 'Anderson's Catalogue of the India Museum,' p. 138.

[2] Described at length in 'Cave Temples of India,' pp. 55–94.

cave. It was consequently indispensable that the two bas-reliefs should be kept separate, which was most artistically effected by the introduction of a panel with no figure sculpture between them. This "stupid blunder" of the cave-architect was more than this, for by his mode of treating this central panel he fortunately has afforded us better means of ascertaining the age of the cave than were otherwise available.

In his excellent 'Catalogue of the Calcutta Museum,' Dr Anderson states, page 147: "The central space is blank, with the exception of a Buddhist rail, with *three chaityas in front of it.*" I was considerably mystified by this assertion, as I had not seen them when I visited the cave, and they do not appear in the lithograph from my sketch, in the first plate of my work on the 'Rock Cut Temples.' I consequently wrote to the Doctor requesting further information,[1] and in reply received a photograph from the cast in the Calcutta Museum of the central panel, which clears up the mystery in a most satisfactory manner. The three objects are not chaityas at all, though they might very easily be mistaken for them, but three pinnacles of a roof which occupies the lower part of the panel in low relief, and is extremely like that depicted by Cunningham, plate xxxi., fig. 4, of the Bharhut Stupa, there described as the throne of the four Buddhas. That, however, has ten pinnacles, very like small chaityas. This roof has only three, like the roof of the Vaitala Deül in the neighbouring city of Bhuvaneswara. Afterwards they became a very favourite ornament, and there is no straight-lined Buddhist roof without them. The so-called Ganesa Rath on Mahavellipur has nine, as shown in the annexed woodcut, and they adorn every Dravidian roof down to the present day. In the Ganesa Cave they are placed so high, almost touching the roof of the verandah, and consequently in such deep shadow that I am not surprised that I did not observe them; and, till I became familiar with the Bharhut sculptures, the idea of representing the image of a roof in this situation did not occur to me.

[1] I fortunately did not allude to the object for which I sought the information, as the Babu might have taken means to prevent my obtaining it, as he has done on other occasions.

The rail which is introduced in the central panel *over* the representation of the roof, is identical with that carved *under* the two sculptured panels on either side of it. It would have been inappropriate below the roof, and therefore to carry out the same decoration throughout, the artist placed it above the roof, behind the pinnacles, so that practically the three panels form a part of one design though varied in detail. I fancy, from its position, there must have been an inscription on this roof—as there is on the throne of the four Buddhas at Bharhut —but probably in paint, and consequently obliterated.

No. 4.—Ganesa Rath, Mahavellipur. (From a Photograph.)

From the position of the roof so represented it is evident that if the cave had been as early as the tope at Bharhut, or of any of the Karli class of caves, the tympana over the doors would have been filled with representations of the wooden framework which invariably fills all the simulated openings at that age. It first ceased to be an obligatory adornment in the sculptures at Sanchi (first century A.D.), only one opening there being so adorned, so far as I can ascertain; and as the tympana in the Ganesa Cave are perfectly plain, in spite of the temptation to adorn them in this manner, I infer that they were executed subsequently to the Sanchi gateways, or say to 100 A.D., or even later.

Everything, in fact, both sculptural and architectural, seems to show that a period, as nearly as can now be ascertained of about three centuries, elapsed between the execution of this cave and that of the Ananta, and, further, that the Ganesa is probably the last Buddhist cave excavated on the Udayagiri hill.

The subject is, however, far from being exhausted. Captain Kittoe's visit, like mine, was too short and hurried to do more than broach the subject which had not been treated archæologically by Stirling or any previous writer. Mr. Locke is the only person who has since then visited the caves with the requisite leisure and all the appliances for compiling an exhaustive description. All the materials, however, which he collected, were placed at the disposal of Babu Rajendralala, and he has made the mess of them that might be expected. Mr. Locke has written nothing regarding them, and we have no means of knowing how far he would have been successful in supplying a satisfactory scientific account had he made the attempt. It is, however, extremely improbable that any European would have invented the silly fables with which the Babu tries to explain the story of the sculptures of Rani-ka-Núr, or would have encumbered his text with the absurd speculations as to the origin of cave architecture, the Babu indulges in at p. 45 of his second volume. The opportunity is, however, lost for the present, and I do not see much chance of its again occurring in my lifetime.

Nothing has occurred since the publication of the work on 'The Cave Temples of India' to throw any fresh light on the subject of the bas-reliefs of the Rani-ka-Núr and the Ganesa Caves, and I am consequently unable to add anything new to what I wrote on the subject in that work (p. 81, *et seq.*). They may all be taken from Buddhist Jatakas, and represent scenes of the 500 previous lives of Buddha. The stories are so various, and, it may be added, so improbable, that without some hint from extraneous sources, it is almost impossible to guess what they are intended to represent, or what their meaning may be. The circumstance, however, that the second bas-relief in the Rani-ka-Núr is repeated without any variation, so far as the story is concerned, in the Ganesa Cave looks very much as if it was some favourite local legend. If it was so favourite a Jataka as to be twice repeated in neighbouring caves, some nearly similar representation would surely have been found at Bharhut or Sanchi, or at Amaravati, or in the Buddhist monasteries in the Eusufsai. As nothing, however, the least like it has been found anywhere, the only chance of explaining its meaning seems to be from a thorough examination of the palm-leaf records of the temple at Puri. Stirling's Pandits extracted so much of the legendary history of the Province from them, that I would not despair of the interpretation of these sculptures being found there also. But for this purpose they must be examined by some one whose mind is free from bias, and who is only anxious to elicit the truth, which does not happen to have been the case when the last examination was undertaken by Babu Rajendralala. He was only anxious to find something which could confute my heresies; which, though a laudable object no doubt, is not sufficient for the purpose.

Although, therefore, the interpretation of these sculptures must, for the present at least, remain a mystery, their age is assuming a certainty which it is extremely improbable that anything that may occur hereafter will disturb. The extreme rudeness of the sculptures of the Ananta Cave, and their general character, prove them to be at the very least as early or even earlier than those of Stupa at Bharhut. Judging from the one photograph we have ('Buddha Gaya,' pl. L.) of the Buddha Gaya sculptures, I should be inclined to rank them with the sculptures there of the age of Asoka, but at all events as the oldest things here. We have only Mr. Beglar's verbal description for the sculptures in the cave that bears his name, but from what he says they must be as old as the Stupa at Bharhut, and if this is so, the caves in the Khandagiri are certainly older than those in the neighbouring hill, and some of them may certainly be dated as before 150 B.C.

On the Udayagiri hill the celebrated Kharavela inscription on the Hathi Gumpha, having a date 146 B.C., makes its age quite certain; and as it is merely a natural cavern, without any attempt at ornament, it probably is the oldest thing there. There is, however, nothing to show why single-celled caves like the Bagh and Sarpa may not be earlier, or even of any date back to the time of Asoka. It may be assumed as certain that the architectural caves, such as the Vaikuntha, the Swargapuri and the Jaya Vijaya, are subsequent, and must range between that date (150 B.C.) and the Christian era. They certainly are all anterior to the Rani-ka-Núr, which is the most splendid of the Katak Caves, and which, from the light recently thrown on the subject, we may certainly assume to have been excavated about the year 1. It may be fifty years before or after that date, but it is hardly necessary to assume so wide a margin, it must approximate very nearly to the Christian era.

For the reasons given above, and the general character of its architecture and sculpture, I have little hesitation in placing the Ganesa Caves at about a century after the Rani-ka-Núr, and, consequently, at about 100 A.D., and about 300 after the Ananta Cave.[1]

[1] At p. 40 of the second volume of the 'Antiquities of Orissa' it is said: "Mr. Fergusson has developed a system of evolution, according to which the simplest of the caves are assigned to the earliest period and the most ornate to a comparatively recent date," &c. I have done nothing of the kind. On the contrary, I have shown that the earliest viharas we know of, are the most ornate both in the east and west. The Ananta Cave in Katak, and the Bhaja Vihara in the Bombay Ghats, 'Cave Temples' (plates xcvi. to xcviii.) are more richly ornamented with sculpture than any subsequent examples known, and if not the oldest, are certainly among the earliest known. It so happens that at Ajunta the earliest caves are the least ornamented, and the later more rich, in paintings especially; but I founded no system upon it, and merely stated the fact, which is of no chronological importance whatever. The age of caves, as of all other buildings, does not depend on their being more or less ornate, but on their *style*, and it is because the Babu has not the smallest idea of the meaning of that word and its application, that is the cause of nine-tenths of the blundering that pervade his books.

There is no *à priori* reason why the date of some of the caves should not extend to the time of Asoka. When that monarch selected the Aswatama rock as a fit place on which to engrave a copy of his famous edicts, in sight of the hills, in which these caves are situated, the place must have been sacred, or at least famous for some reason or other. It may consequently then or immediately afterwards have been selected as a residence for cenobites, or persons devoted to the new faith, which was then becoming the established religion of the country.

The limit the other way depends wholly on the style of the architecture and sculpture of the caves, which enable us to determine it with very tolerable certainty. The Buddhists ceased to excavate caves on the east side of India long before they abandoned the practice in the west, owing apparently to the circumstance that the rocks on the east were far less adapted for the purpose than the trap formations of the west. The granite rocks of Behar were too hard for the purpose, and with the exception of the sandstone hills of the Udayagiri, it is difficult to find any suitable rocks on the eastern side of India, while the whole of the Bombay Presidency is covered with volcanic rocks singularly well suited for the purpose.

Having so recently as 1880[1] written so full an account of these caves, there would have been no occasion for again treating of the subject, were it not for a desire to free the subject from some of the errors which the writings of the Babu have introduced into the discussion, and to add what few facts have come to light in the meanwhile. The discovery of a date 146 B.C. in the famous Hathi Gumpha inscription throws a flood of light on the subject, and gives a precision to our reasonings that they did not before possess. It may now be assumed that none of the caves on the Udayagiri—even those where the sculpture is confined to the tympana—can be ascribed to a much earlier date; but this is not quite so clear with regard to those on the Khan-

[1] 'Cave Temples of India,' pp. 55 to 94.

dagiri. There are no reasons derivable from the character of their sculptures why such caves as the Ananta and Beglar's Cave should not be carried back some fifty or even a hundred years—say even to Asoka's time, or very nearly so—but it would require the personal examination of some competent person before this could be settled.

It is possible, I may say probable, that the Dagoba, which almost certainly formed part of the group, stood on the summit of Khandagiri hill, where the Jaina temple now stands, and that the Deva Sabha is a reminiscence of its previous existence. If this could be established, it would account for earliest caves having been excavated in that hill.

CHAPTER III.

BHUVANESWARA.

If Babu Rajendralala cannot be congratulated on the use he made of the materials furnished to him by Mr. Locke for the description of the Katak Caves, he seems to have been even less successful with those collected by his "personally conducted" expedition to Bhuvaneswara, which, in some respects, is almost equally to be regretted. Owing to its remoteness from the seats of Muhammadan power, the province almost entirely escaped the ravages which devastated the principal Hindu cities in the early and more intolerant age of their power. The conquest of Orissa was only made in 1510 by Husain Shah, the king of Bengal, and was held by the Bengal kings with a very uncertain grasp, when it was rescued from them by the tolerant Akbar in 1574, after which no further outrages were to be feared. In consequence of this, the Hindu monuments are more nearly intact than any other group in the north of India. Except at Jajepur, which afterwards the Muhammadans made their capital and where they built a mosque, it is astonishing how little damage was done by them. Neither at Bhuvaneswara, nor at Puri, nor at Konaruc, can any trace of Muhammadan violence be found. Not a nose is knocked off, nor an image overthrown. The only injury that has been done has been by the antiquarian zeal of such men as Colonel Mackenzie and General Stewart,[1] who removed some of the best statues of the Raj Rani, and by the vandals who pulled down and attempted to remove the Nava Graha from the Temple of Konaruc. They have also suffered from the sordid proceedings of the Public Works Department, which destroyed the fort of Barbati and

[1] 'Antiquities of Orissa,' vol. ii. p. 90.

other public buildings of the province to mend roads, or to save some money in erecting a light-house at False Point.

Besides their immunity from the ordinary causes of destruction of Hindu buildings, the Orissa group forms in itself one of the most complete and interesting in all India. The Khajeraho group is nearly as extensive and magnificent, but they were all erected within the limits of one century, 950 to 1050 A.D.,[1] so that no sequence can be traced among them. There are also temples in Dharwar and Mysore more magnificent than any in Orissa, and extending through a longer series of years; but they are scattered over a wide extent of country, and are consequently varied by local peculiarities of style. It consequently requires more knowledge and more experience to classify them than it does those in this province. Altogether there is not, perhaps, any group which, if properly investigated, would add more to our knowledge of Indian architecture and give it more precision than the Bhuvaneswara temples. It was, therefore, a gratuitous piece of blundering to entrust the task to one who, though an excellent Sanscrit scholar, knew nothing of either architecture or archæology, and who thoroughly despised the doctrines of the latter science, which would have enabled him to extract some meaning from what he saw. With the unlimited breadth of text and wealth of illustration that were placed at his disposal,[2] he might easily have given us a monograph of Orissan buildings that would have filled up one of the greatest lacunæ in our Indian artistic history. As it is, he has written a book which will be a perplexity to all future generations of explorers who may have occasion to consult it, and which conveys, if I mistake not, as little real information to its readers, as any work of the same pretension in modern times.

The Babu begins the description of the Orissan temples by

[1] 'Cunningham's Reports,' vol. ii. p. 416.

[2] If the Bengal Government had allowed General Cunningham a half, or a fraction indeed, of the same wealth of illustration that they have allowed the Babu, we might by this time have had an accumulation of facts regarding Indian archæology, which would have been of the greatest value for the illustration of the subject, whatever may have been the deductions he might have drawn from them. As it is, his volumes are printed on the worst possible paper, and his illustrations of the most meagre description.

the compilation of the following table, which may be taken as a fair sample of the book, though it puzzles me, and I fancy will most people, to find out what his object in compiling was :—[1]

NAME.	Outer Measurement.	Inner Measurement.	Total Area.	Area of Room.	Ratio of Solids to the Total Area; in Decimals.	Ratio of Room to the Total Area; in Decimals.	Nearest Vulgar Fraction.
Bhagavatí ..	38×38	13×13	1,444	169	·882	·117	1/10
Great Tower ..	66×60	42×42	3,960	1,764	·554	·445	4/9
Rámes'vara ..	34×34	16×16	1,156	256	·778	·221	2/9
Paras'urames'vara	20×20	11× 9	400	99	·752	·247	1/4
Yames'vara ..	22×22	12×12	484	144	·702	·297	2/7
Kapiles'vara ..	20×16	9× 9	320	81	·746	·253	1/4
Rájarán'i	32×25	12×12	800	144	·820	·180	1/5
Muktes'vara ..	14×14	6× 6	196	36	·816	·183	1/5
Puri	73×73	29×29	5,239	841	·842	·158	1/6
Sarideül	24×22	12×12	528	144	·727	·272	3/11
Somes'vara ..	23×23	11×11	529	121	·772	·228	2/9
Ananta-vásudeva	26×26	16×14	696	224	·678	·322	1/3

As the cellas of all Hindu temples are absolutely dark—none have a window in them—their votaries never being admitted to them on any ceremonious occasions, their Æsthetic proportions cannot be of the least possible consequence. Nor can construction; in all instances sufficient stability could easily be provided for, and was so, without interfering with any artistic or constructive exigency, so that their proportions required no table to explain them. The table does not pretend that any diminution or extension of the area of the voids compared w th those of the solids, marks an improvement in constructive skill, or artistic taste, which could lead to the detection of any progress in any direction. It cannot consequently tend to the formation of any sequence which could lead to the determination of the dates of the temple, or in fact could convey any information either of construction or chronology. If it were not to exhibit the Babu's knowledge of vulgar and decimal fractions, I do not know for what motive it was compiled—and certainly he does not explain why it was done. Though, however, it may answer this purpose of airing his arithmetical skill, it would have been well for the

[1] 'Antiquities of Orissa,' vol. i., Calcutta, 1875, p. 41.

Babu's reputation that it had been omitted, for in addition to the errors inherent to a table compiled from the wretched plans in his work (vol. ii. pls. xlviii. and xlix.), it required a more than usual amount of ingenuity to compile one which must, *ex hypothesi*, be wrong in every item.

All the cells of Hindu temples, or nearly all, are plain square apartments, without ornament; their dimensions are consequently easily obtained when admission is allowed to them, which is nearly always impossible to foreigners—in temples still in use—and not always easy to natives. Their length multiplied by their breadth will, consequently, always give the area of the

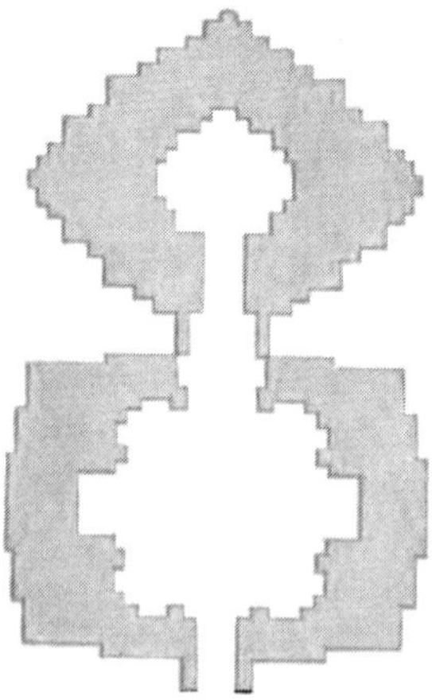

No. 5.—Rajarani Temple, Bhuvaneswara. (From 'Antiquities of Orissa,' vol. ii. Plate xlix.) Scale, 30 feet to 1 inch.

voids. But I think I may assert that there is not a single Hindu temple of any importance in India whose base, externally, is so bounded; I cannot at least call one to mind. In all instances the outline of the base is broken by projections more or less pronounced. Sometimes not much beyond a straight line, though sometimes assuming a star shape, but varying between these two extremes into a variety of forms, but never such that the simple proportion of length to breadth can give the dimension with any desired degree of exactness. Take for instance the Rajarani—the seventh in the table—it would puzzle any moderate mathematician to show how 12 × 12 could describe the voids and 32 × 35, the solids of the temple. A much more elaborate set of figures are wanted for the purpose; but it is hardly worth while to attempt it, as the photographs prove the plan to be so intolerably incorrect that it ought to be rejected altogether. When I was writing the 'History of Indian Architecture,' I attempted to draw one from the photographs, and produced the accompanying woodcut. It is certainly more like the temple, but any one who knows how difficult it is to draw plans, with no other materials than photographs of the building, will not be surprised it is not quite to be relied upon. It is better at all events than the Babu's, said to be made on the spot, which, in its squeezed-up form, I will venture to say is not like any temple ever erected by Hindu hands.

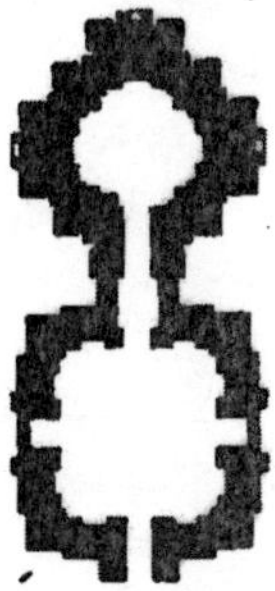

No. 6.—Temple of Rajarani. (Compiled from Photographs.) Scale 50 ft. to 1 in.

One might easily forgive the Babu his distortion of the plan of the Rajarani temple, if he had provided us with a correct one of the great temple itself, which is the principal feature in the book, and the most interesting of all the existing Orissan temples. In the above table the tower is described as 66 feet by 60, while all the photographs prove that it is undoubtedly square, and from the mode on which its Amla sila, or Amalaka is set upon it, it could not possibly be otherwise. Indeed, the Babu seems to be aware of this, for further on he says (p. 75): "The body of the tower is about fifty-five feet high, and, omitting the side projections, forms a cube on the ground plan." Whatever this may mean, it seems to intimate that the four sides at least were equal. In the plan they are represented as 66 by 54 feet from angle to angle, and the internal dimensions are in the table quoted as 42 square. In the plan they are 43 by 46, and approach so nearly to the exterior, that if the tower had been built, as represented in the plan, it would not have stood for an hour, much less for 1200 years as it has now done. When I attempted to correct this plan,[1] I reduced the internal dimension to 40 feet, with the larger external one of 65 feet, and so made it constructively

[1] 'History of Indian Architecture,' woodcut 232.

possible. If I were to draw it again, my conviction is, that the interior dimensions must be nearer 30 than 40 feet, probably even less, and so I feel sure it will be found when any one who can measure, visits it. The great temple at Puri, which is a larger one than this, and whose cella is built to accommodate three images, is only 30 feet square, and other temples have cells of about the same proportion.

The other parts of the temple are nearly, though not quite so incorrectly represented, as the great tower. The Bhoja mantapa is said in the text (p. 72) to be 56 feet square. By the scale it is 64 by 70. The Natmandir is said in the text to be 52 feet square, and scales 58 by 60. The most correctly described portion is the Mohan, which in the text is said to measure 65 feet by 45 on the plan. It measures 70 by 50; but some allowance must be made from the impossibility of my taking dimensions, from plans on so small a scale, with absolute exactness. It is only the grossest errors that can be with certainty detected.

Making these and all the other adjustments obtainable from the plan, it reduces the total length to about 210 feet, instead of the 290 of the plan, and this I feel sure is nearly the correct measurement. This corrected dimension is confirmed by Mr. Atkinson's plan (plate xxviii.), which has been made by a much more accurate surveyor than the Babu or any of his assistants can pretend to be.[1] In like manner the Temple of Bhagavati (plate xlviii.), which looks more like a correct representation of a Hindu temple than any other plan in the Babu's book, is represented as 160 feet in length, while Mr. Atkinson makes it only 110, which I fancy is very much nearer the truth.

The other thirteen plans contained in volume ii. are of less importance, but are certainly as incorrect, both in form and in dimension, as those just quoted, though from the absence of photographs these discrepancies are not always easy of

[1] I possess a tracing of this plan of Mr. Atkinson's, to nearly three times the scale of that engraved in the Babu's book, and from this I am able to check the dimensions of the Babu's plans, but even then it is on too small a scale to be relied upon implicitly.

detection, and where they are, the temples are too insignificant to make it worth while to point them out.

There is one point in which these plans, notwithstanding these defects, might have been made to afford useful information had the Babu had the wit to supply it, and would have cost very little trouble. Had he adopted a different tone of shading to distinguish what were parts of the original design and what were added afterwards, it would have rendered their history infinitely more intelligible than it now is. A regular Orissan temple consists of a tower over the cella, and a mohan or porch in front of it, and of these parts only. Nine-tenths of them retain this double form to the present day. In front of the great temples, however, there was erected a detached Bhoga mantapa, to which the image of the god was removed on the occasion of certain festivals, and where he was worshipped and offerings made to him more conveniently than could be done in the cella under the dewal, or tower. Afterwards, in some instances, this mantapa was joined to the mohan by a natmandir, or dancing hall, generally a very much lower, and every way an inferior building, but thus making up the fourfold temple sometimes found in Orissa.[1] It certainly was the case in the great temple at Bhuvaneswara, where the Bhoga mantapa was added by Kemala Kesari in 792 to 811, and the natmandir by Salini Kesari in 1099 to 1104. It was the case in the temple at Puri, where the Bhoga mantapa formerly existing at Konaruc was transported to adorn that temple by the Mahrattas in the last century, and the natmandir inserted afterwards to join the two together. At Konaruc it was a detached porch. There is evidence that it never was joined to the mohan, and in the two or three temples in which the fourfold arrangement exists, it is evident it is an addition. In the Kapileswara (plate xlv.) this is seen at a glance from the difference of style, and in the Ananta Vasu deva it is evidently so, though I have no photograph that shows the lower parts of the temple with sufficient distinctness to prove it. The inscription, however,

[1] On two occasions Mr. Hunter twits me for not appreciating this fourfold division of Orissan temples ('Orissa,' vol. i. pp. 132–289). My belief is that in all instances it is an accidental accretion, never a part of the original design.

quoted by the Babu (page 85) is nearly sufficient for the purpose. The date is near the end of the eleventh century (1075 ?), and cannot possibly apply to a building of about the same age as the great temple, but it may apply to some buildings added to it afterwards. The word translated "temple," by Major Marshall, is "prâsâda," which can hardly mean a temple, properly so called, but may mean a mantapa of any kind, and certainly seems to do so in this instance.

In tower-like buildings, such as these Orissan temples always are, it is nearly as important to ascertain their heights as it is their plans, in order to understand their construction and to appreciate the effect. The Babu seems to have been perfectly aware of this, and he certainly cannot be blamed for neglecting it, though he seems to have been as unsuccessful in determining the heights of the temples as he was in measuring their plans, though this arose from different causes. In the first place, he neglects to define what parts are included in the height. Was it the domelike summit of the tower? or did it include the kalasa, or vase-like termination, by which they are invariably crowned? or does it also include the trident or chackra of metal, which some would include in the height? Till this is determined, it is of course in vain to attempt any precision. My impression is that it ought to include the kalasa, but to exclude any metal-work, or flag-staff, which sometimes adds considerably to its elevation and to its appearance. But leaving this question to be determined hereafter, in the first attempt the Babu made to ascertain the height of the Bhuvaneswara tower he ought to have been successful. He sent up a man, a sort of "Steeple Jack," with his measuring-tape, to ascertain the height by actual measurement. If the tape was, however, an ordinary one of only 60 feet in length, this would not be so easy as it looks, especially to a man who cannot read the figures. With so broken an outline as the upper parts of these towers always have, the various parts must be measured separately, and added together afterwards. By this means he satisfied himself that the height was 160 feet, and originally 165 to the top of the kalasa—specified in this instance (p. 75). Mr. Eastwick, employing the same means, and, apparently, the same man, came to the conclusion that the height to the top of the dome was 127 feet, and that the kalasa *with the trident* was 34, making the whole 161 feet.[1] We have only therefore to ascertain the height of the kalasa to reconcile the two accounts. Unfortunately this is not so easy. On plate xxxiv., vol. i., n. 151, the Babu gives a representation of a kalasa; whilst on page 75, vol. ii., is said to be that of the great tower, which the photographs show it certainly is not, and even then there is no scale. No. 152 on the same plate is more like it, but at page 110 of the first volume is said to be from the temple of Yameswara, so that will not help us. From the photographs I fancy the kalasa of the great tower is about one-tenth of the whole height, say 13 feet, which would make the total height 140 feet, which is certainly 10 feet too low. Mr. Eastwick's 127 feet appears to be the height of the square part of the tower, which the "Steeple Jack" would naturally make his first measurement. The photographs show the 34 feet is at least 10 feet in excess, so that the real result is that the tower is 150 in height, including the kalasa, which, curiously enough, is the amount figured on the plan of the temple on plate xlviii. of the second volume of the 'Antiquities of Orissa.'

The Babu was not, however, satisfied in his own mind by these measurements. He "ascertained the height by taking angles from three different places" (p. 75); and in like manner at Puri, where he had no "Steeple Jack" to help him, he found the height had been raised from the 160 at Bhuvaneswara to 192 feet. He adds, page 116: "The last was ascertained by me from angles taken from different distances." Was it? It would be rude to say the Babu did not make these observations, but it would be extremely interesting to know with what kind of instrument they were made. Was it a theodolite? or a sextant? and how were the base lines measured? If a temple stands alone on the plain, it is very easy to measure a base line from its centre or side, and with any sort of goniometer to ascertain the height by trigonometry. But when a temple

[1] Murray's 'Handbook of Bengal,' p. 124.

is situated in a courtyard, surrounded by high walls, and crowded with temples and buildings of all sorts, it has always seemed to me nearly impossible to measure a base line from it to any distance sufficient to get a view of its kalasa. Outside the courtyard no doubt plain spaces may be found, but then it requires that two angles should be observed, and then an ill-conditioned triangle is obtained, very difficult to measure or to protract; and in no case, in those conditions, can the base and the summit be seen from the same spot, so that even when a sextant is used, the height of the place of observation must be ascertained before that of the temple can be observed.

In fact, the difficulties of using trigonometry to ascertain the height of these two temples appear to me nearly insuperable, without, at least, far more time and more delicate appliances than I fancy the Babu or any of his staff could apply to the purpose. Certainly the result is not satisfactory. I do not believe the tower is 192 feet, including the kalasa. In the rooms of the Asiatic Society there is an elaborate elevation of this temple, drawn to scale, and with a scale attached to it. This makes the tower, the top of the dome, 152 feet, and the kalasa, with the *metal chakra*, 30 feet, or 182 total height. It is only a native drawing, and consequently not quite to be depended upon; but as the horizontal dimensions work out correctly, according to Radhikaprasnad Mukerji's[1] plan, I have confidence in the elevation, which is also confirmed by the photographs. It is true the Babu professes to have ascertained the height to within 21 inches by a comparison of its proportions with those of the Bhuvaneswara tower; but as these last were not ascertained within a limit of 10 feet, either horizontically or vertically, and as he takes the central sections through the buttresses, which made the width 80 feet, instead of the elevation 66 feet from angle to angle, which I would have taken, I do not see how any satisfactory rule of three can be worked out. From such vague premises any height may be obtained, and none that would be satisfactory. In fact I do not believe that any law of proportion between Orissa temples has been discovered. Taking, for instance, those on plate xlix., we

[1] 'Antiquities of Orissa,' vol. ii. Plate 51.

have Mukteswara's horizontal diameter 16 feet, height 36, or more than double; Someswara 25, height 67, or more than twice and a half; Parasurameswara 21, height 38, or less than twice; Bhagavati 40 feet, 54; and Ananta Vasa deva 30 feet, height 60, which probably, on the whole, is what the Orissan architects really intended—to make the height twice the diameter, though from various causes—it may be from the incorrectness of the Babu's plans—they never seem exactly to have accomplished it. If they did aim at it, and varied it according to age, it would be interesting, if we had the data for ascertaining it; but I am afraid the plans of the 'Antiquities of Orissa' are too incorrect for any theory to be based upon them. This is to be regretted, for if the Babu had put aside all trigonometrical observations and elaborate calculations, there was a very simple means available, by which the heights could have been ascertained easily with quite sufficient accuracy for our purposes. He had only to attach a graduated 10-foot surveying rod to the face of each temple, before photographing it, and he would have obtained a scale sufficient for all purposes. To one who could observe angles with such readiness it may have appeared too simple, but to an outsider it would have been more satisfactory.

There is of course in the 'Antiquities of Orissa' no attempt to arrange the temples in any order, either chronologically or even as to form. Such an attempt at classification would be entirely unworthy of one who looks on the science of archæology with such contempt; but, what is worse for his readers, no attempt has been made to arrange his plates in any intelligible order. As they came from the lithographer they were placed in the book, without the least reference either to style or locality; and, as he also adopts the slovenly practice of not writing any names or descriptions on the plates, it requires a steady head and a good memory to utilise them to any extent.

The plates in the first volume begin well, with an elevation to scale of a singularly interesting though exceptional temple, but so well drawn by a student of the School of Art, Kali Das Pal, that we cannot help regretting that it is the only one of its class. The more so that it is only of the back of the temple, which is the least interesting face, and the one that tells least of its story. As there is no plan and no section, I defy any one who has not access to other means of information than those supplied by this work, to understand its peculiarities. A photograph taken from the point of view from which I sketched it in 1837[1] would have told its story far more completely, and one might easily have been spared.[2] There are, for instance, in the second volume two views, plates xxix. and xxxi., which are duplicates of one another. The one is taken from the steps of a temple called in the map the temple of Someswara. The other from the edge of a tank a little in front of it, but the two photographs comprehend the same temples, and from exactly the same point of view. I can perfectly understand the uneducated eye of the Babu not perceiving this, but it is so, the one being only a little nearer the great tower than the other, so that one might very well have been spared. It does not help the matter to describe one in the list of the plates that is inserted in the text as a "View of the Great Tower from the *North-east*," the other as a "View of the same from the *North-west*," the latter being the true description of both. Or, if expense was any object, plate vii. might very well have been omitted. It represents the pillars of an insignificant pavilion in the courtyard of the great temple at Puri, which have no connection with any building or style represented in any other part of the work. They belong to a style of architecture introduced after the reign of Akbar, and common enough at Mathura or Benares, but not found, so far as I know, elsewhere in Orissa, and why introduced in this place passes my understanding.

There are other illustrations of the temple of Vaitala Deül, which, if judiciously selected, might have added much to our knowledge. Plate xviii. contains two female figures, which are already sufficiently illustrated in plate ii. It would have been far more interesting to have given Durga slaying the

[1] 'Picturesque illustrations of Ancient architecture in Hindostan,' plate iv.

[2] Two were taken by the photographers of the expedition.—Vide Appendix A. I cannot identify them among the twelve I possess of this temple.

Maha Asura, from the centre of the north front, so as to enable us to compare it with the sculptures representing the same subject at Mahavellipur [1] and Elura. Or they might have re-drawn the central figure, which the lithographer has represented as a woman, while it really is Siva as Ardanari.

According to the list published in the Appendix, two photographs were taken, which, even if they partially represented the front, would have shown that the central bas-relief over the porch represented Surya, with his two wives, drawn in his chariot by seven horses, which at this age became the usual number. In his 'Orissa' Mr. Hunter mentions a similar piece of sculpture as existing at Jajepur (pages 271, 285), which unfortunately I did not see, and have no photograph of; but this constantly recurring representation of the Sun-god is of singular interest, as leading up to the temple of Konaruc (the Black Pagoda), which is the most beautiful and most important temple dedicated to sun-worship to be found in India.

I have very great doubts in my own mind whether the Babu ever visited this temple of Vaitala Deül. Report says he did not. Otherwise it is strange he should not have remarked some of these peculiarities, and inconceivable that he should not have seen the mohan of the Merkandeswar [2] temple close alongside of it—within at least ten yards, and certainly of about the same age. If he did, he certainly never could have said that the portico of the Vaitala Deül and that of the Parasu Rameswara (page 93) are the only two similar edifices to be found at Bhuvaneswara. Though at page 95 he describes this porch as of the *usual* Orissa form, he merely means *un*usual, for as he had just said there were only two of this class, while there are hundreds of the class of those of the great temple, the two must be characterised as of the

[1] Transactions of the R. A. S., vol. ii. plate iv.

[2] I have great doubts as to the name of this temple. It is so called in one of my photographs, but I have reason to believe Markandesvara is applied to a temple situated at some distance from this. But the names are often most incorrectly written on my photographs, and as the Babu's descriptions are often so inexact, it is almost impossible to avoid making mistakes in naming them.

exceptional form. There are three at least, and the porch of the Markandeswara is the most beautiful of them. It has the processions along the outer edge of the roof, which gives such richness of effect to the roofs of the great temple, to that at Konaruc, and, so far as I know, are only found there. Its whole details make it a gem of Orissan art, though in a sadly ruined state.

Throughout his work on Orissa the Babu persists in calling this temple Vaitala Deül—which certainly is not the name by which it is known to the Brahmins or any one else. If, however, he had called it Kapila Devi, or Kapileswara, or any such name, he would have been obliged to acknowledge that he had seen the plate I published of it in 1846, and to confess that in the few hours I passed at Bhuvaneswara, I had done more to convey to outsiders a correct notion of this temple and its peculiarities than he had done after a long sojourn there, with all his array of draftsmen and casters. Fortunately, however, all his assistants were not moved by the same petty jealousies as their chief. Ten casts were taken and two drawings which are entered under the designation of "Temple of Kopaleswari" (see Appendix A), and in Dr. Anderson's Catalogue of the Calcutta Museum they are entered under the title of "Kapilesvara." But as that name in the Babu's book applies only to a temple a mile away from Bhuvaneswara—from which no casts were taken—the confusion is as great as in most other parts of the Babu's book.

With regard to the Rajarani it is even worse. In Mr. Locke's list in the Appendix, 18 casts of subjects were taken, but as one of these was the mysterious minaret, in twelve pieces, the total number of casts was 30 or 32, according as we count subjects or casts to make up the 132 casts, making 119 subjects. In Dr. Anderson's Catalogue we have 30 subjects—47 to 77—without the "minaret." Without seeing the casts themselves, it seems impossible, at present, to reconcile the 18 casts of Mr. Locke's list in the Appendix, with the 30 of Dr. Anderson's Catalogue. The only way of accounting for it, that occurs to me, is that 10 and 12 squeezes from other temples have got labelled in error, and so make up the tale. Whether this is the correct explanation of the difficulty or not, it is curiously characteristic of the Babu's work, that 20 or 30 casts should have been taken from one temple and no measurements or diagrams should have been made to show from what part of the temple they were taken, or what their use or juxtaposition was. He had artists with him who could easily have supplied this deficiency—if he had felt the want of it. But he did not, and his casts are consequently absolutely worthless for any scientific purpose. For any object that I can understand they would have been far better replaced by an equal number of photographs, at a fraction of the expense and infinitely more easily available for students.

It would be as tedious as unprofitable to attempt to criticise the plates of detail given in the Babu's first volume. They were selected without the guidance of any fixed principle, and are arranged on no intelligible system. Nor is it possible, even if we should cut up the book into separate pages, to arrange them as I did the casts at South Kensington, according to the temples from which they are taken, to gain any archæological information from the plates. I would only remark in passing that No. 29, pl. xiii., is not from the great tower as described. It evidently is not an Orissan example at all, but taken from some temple in Dharwar or in the south-west of India, though how it got here is by no means clear. In like manner it would be easy, if worth while, to criticise the selection of photographs of temples in the second volume. They are all too much of one type, and not the best or most interesting of their class. There are others, as the Gauri Devi (query as to name) which are as exceptional in form as the Vaitala Deül, and consequently as suggestive of foreign relationship, and as beautiful in detail, as the Mukteswara, but which remain in this collection entirely unrepresented. From my own collection of photographs I fancy I could have made a very much better and more typical selection; but, as the Babu had no system and no story to tell, one photograph in his eyes was as good as another, and we must be grateful for what we have got. The photographs of the temple at Konaruc, lvi., lvii., and lxiii., which are about the most interesting and valuable in the work, are barely sufficient to do justice to this, which even in its ruined state is one of the most beautiful and interesting temples in Orissa.

When I last had occasion to write about this temple, in my 'History of Indian Architecture' (1876), I was so much struck with the apparent impossibility of the Orissan architects being able to produce so exquisite a specimen of their art—the most beautiful in the province—after perpetrating such an abomination as the Temple of Jugganât at Puri, that I rejected unhesitatingly the received date for the Konaruc temple (1241 A.D.). I then placed it at 850 A.D., from a date incidentally quoted by Abul Fazl,[1] who is the principal authority for the more modern one. Since then, with more photographs and a more careful investigation of all the details, I am inclined to go even further in this direction, though I have, I admit, no written authority for so doing; but relying wholly on archæological data, I feel inclined to place it nearly a century earlier.

Assuming the great temple at Bhuvaneswara to have been built 667 A.D., and comparing it with the mohan at Konaruc, it shows just such progress of design as one might expect in about a century. It is lighter and more elegant in outline, and there is progress towards that style of decoration which was fully developed in the tower of the Rajarani (900 ?), though still a long way from the style of that temple.

What, however, I most rely upon is its similarity with the details of ornamentation with the Mukteswara, which appear to me only slightly more modern than the great tower. It was erected before these temples lost their square form, so characteristic of Orissan architecture of the best age, but when the tendency to excessive elaboration and ornament was most conspicuous. In the Mukteswara (pl. xxxiii.) there is an ornament runs round the windows, which is very peculiar, and, so far as I can make out, does not occur anywhere after, say, the eighth or ninth centuries. It is represented in plates iii. and in xii. fig. 28 *b*, and also xxxvi. fig. 143. It occurs also surrounding the doorway at Konaruc, plate lvii., with so little variation

[1] 'Ayeen Akbaree,' Gladwin's translation, vol. ii. p. 16.

that it may be called identical, and with accompaniments so similar in style that, if they were not, they might easily be executed by the same masons. The moulding occurs also surrounding the doorway of Cave 23 at Ajunta, in a slightly more ancient form, but with accompaniments so similar to those at Konaruc that they cannot be very far distant in date; and as the cave belongs without any doubt to the seventh century, it cannot well be brought down lower than the eighth and ninth. It occurs also in a temple at Desgarh in Central India, of which General Cunningham has sent me some photographs. He, I know, places the temple at about the same age as the cave, and, from internal evidence, I fancy he is nearly right; but none of these buildings can, if there is any truth in archæology, be brought down at all events to the ninth century.[1]

No. 7.—Ornament from Doorway of Cave 23 Ajunta (from a photograph).

This may be all very well in an archæological sense, but, as it is avowedly a *theory* of mine, it must from the Babu's point of view be wrong *ex hypothesi*; and as his mission is to contradict whatever I assert and to expose my errors, this could not be passed over. It was not easy for the Babu to do this on archæological grounds, because he had not sufficient familiarity with its doctrines or data. Some other means had to be discovered for doing so. He consequently undertook to prove from the 'Palm-leaf Records' of the temple at Puri—to which he might feel perfectly certain I could in no circumstances gain access—that the temple which we now see is a very different affair from what it was when erected by Anang Bhim Deva in 1174–1198. From these records he extracted the following paragraphs[2]:—

"For some time after the erection of the temple no necessity was felt for repairs, and nothing was attempted beyond slight touching up of breaks and accidental injuries; but, sub-

[1] It is also figured in the 'Buddha Gaya,' plate xlviii., from an example from Nalanda of uncertain date, but probably tenth century.

[2] 'Antiquities of Orissa,' vol. ii. p. 117.

sequently, the destruction caused by repeated Moslem assaults rendered thorough repairs unavoidable. According to the 'Temple Records,' the first thorough repairs to the temple were executed in the reign of Pratáparadra (A.D. 1504 to 1532), when, it is distinctly stated, the temple was 'plastered and whitewashed.' Nrisinha Deva repeated the operation in 1647. During the reign of Krishna Deva (A.D. 1713 to 1718), soon after a Muhammadan assault, thorough repairs were again necessitated. And fifty years later the queen of Virakis'ora Deva gave the fourth general repairs. Besides these, partial repairs frequently had to be resorted to. In fact the purification of the temple after every Muhammadan assault included a whitewashing, which, however beneficial as a lustration, told seriously against the delicate carved work, and its frequent repetition completed the ruin of the temple as a work of art.

"The injury so done is irreparable. It has converted a monument scarcely inferior, from an art point of view, to the great tower of Bhuvanes'vara, and quite as sumptuously carved as the Black Pagoda, into an ugly mass of stones. It has led, however, to inferences about the decay of Indian art which are by no means justifiable. Mr. Fergusson, adverting to the absence of detail, says: 'The degradation of the faith, however, is hardly so remarkable as that of the style. Even Stirling, who was no captious critic, remarks that it seems unaccountable in an age when the architects obviously possessed some taste and skill, and were, in most cases, particularly lavish in the use of sculptural ornament, so little pains should have been taken with the decoration and finishing of this sacred and stupendous edifice.[1] It is not, however, in the detail, but the outline, the proportions, and every arrangement of the temple, show that the art in this province at least had received a fatal downward impetus from which it never recovered.'"

The first thing that strikes one as peculiar in reading this is, that Stirling's pandits, who examined these records with care, make no mention of these Moslem outrages—nor does Bhabanicharan Bandopadhyaya, if we may trust Mr. Hunter's

[1] 'Asiatic Researches,' vol. xv. p. 315.

analysis of his work—which I have not seen; but he found nothing of the sort in the Purushottama Chandrika.[1] Indeed, the boast of the priests when I was there, and I have understood always was, that the foot of no Kafir or Faringhi had ever polluted their sacred precincts. I do not fancy his countrymen will be particularly grateful for the Babu's exposure of this fallacy; and certain it is, that if they did so desecrate the interior, they did not touch the exterior. The figures that adorn the outer gateway in the market-place are still untouched; not a nose knocked off, nor an arm broken. But further, if we consider what these incursions involved, it will appear how impossible this account of them should be true. An army of Kafirs, however strong and numerous, taking possession of a temple, and bent on desecrating it, could only injure statues and mouldings to a height of 6 or 8 feet. To injure and alter the appearance of a tower 150 to 200 feet high, and with walls 25 feet in thickness, they must have erected heavy scaffolding, and employed an army of masons working for a considerable time. It is not pretended that they did this, and the proof that they did not is that the sculptures of the great tower and all its ornaments are exactly as they were when originally erected. I have seen them, and can vouch for this, and though my testimony would of course be rejected by the Babu, there are abundance of photographs which cannot lie; the Babu's own plate liii. is nearly sufficient for this purpose. The difficulty is, however, that it is nearly impossible to bring the camera near enough for the purpose. My woodcut (No. 238) is clearer, but even it is not satisfactory. They are, however, quite sufficient to prove that the tower now stands as first erected, and that its sculptures and ornaments are quite uninjured. It may at some period have been whitewashed, though there is no evidence of this, and tropical rains of a single season generally suffices to cure that vulgarity. Of the mohan I cannot speak from personal observation; it is not visible from the outside, and I have no sufficient photograph to judge from. The Bhoga Mantapa, as explained above, was brought from Konaruc, and is in a style intermediate between

[1] 'Hunter's Orissa,' vol. i. p. 199.

the two temples to which it alternately belonged, and the natmandir is even more modern; but both the parts were erected here subsequently to the Moslem outrages. I presume that, even with his slight knowledge of architectural styles, the Babu will hardly deny that the Bhoga mantapa (plate lv.), brought from Konaruc, is older than the building to which it is now attached; but if this is so, there is an end of the controversy. If the Bhoga mantapa is older than the building at Puri, which it certainly is, and from its detached position in front of the Black Pagoda, where it was originally erected, it was certainly more modern than the temple itself, it follows as a matter of course that the Black Pagoda at Konaruc must be more ancient than the temple at Puri. How much more so, is the only question. I think at least four centuries, but that remains to be settled by further inquiries; but meanwhile the Babu's contention that it is more modern is manifestly absurd, and if the 'Temple Records' do really contain the information Babu Rajendralala states that he extracted from them in the above paragraph, the facts and the photographs are quite sufficient to prove how utterly unreliable they are.

My conviction is, however, that the 'Palm-leaf Records' do not say what the Babu represents them as recording, and that it is only that he has read them with distorted spectacles, determined to see in them only what could contradict me and controvert my pernicious theories; but in doing so it appears to me he has only desecrated in the eyes of his countrymen their most sacred temple, which was always hitherto considered inviolate, and thrown discredit on one of the most cherished traditions of his people, without in the smallest degree altering the facts of the case. If the conclusions arrived at by the science of archæology from the study of the buildings themselves can be sustained, the whole is clear and consecutive, and no special pleading or production of irrelevant or suspicious testimony can alter them in the slightest degree.

As mentioned above, there is no attempt in the 'Antiquities of Orissa' to arrange the temples in any sort of sequence according to their dates, or even to group them in classes according to their forms or details. To do this would have required study, and at least some elementary knowledge of the science of archæology, for which the Babu has such supreme contempt. There are no inscriptions which are integral, or which state with any kind of distinctness that certain buildings, or portions of them, were erected at any time which can be ascertained from a date in the inscription, or in which, from the form of its characters, its date could be fixed within any moderate limits. If, in short, the date or position in the sequence could not be ascertained from the style, the attempt was nearly hopeless, at least in the present state of our information. I have often fancied that the 'Temple Records' of Puri might supply the deficiency, but they have never been examined for the purpose. I have not seen the Purushottama Chandrika, but so far as I gather from Mr. Hunter's account of it, its author felt no interest in architecture in any form, and it would require some special knowledge to abstract intelligently from them the information on this subject they may contain. In spite of the slur thrown on their authenticity by the use that has been made of them by Babu Rajendra in the extract quoted above, I believe, from the authentic information gleaned from them by Stirling's Pandits and others, that they may contain a mine of useful information on this subject also.

I have on several occasions attempted classification of these temples, but avowedly merely tentative, in order to attract attention to the subject, in hopes that some one with more knowledge would do better. I have nothing but photographs to depend upon, and for this purpose they are most unsatisfactory. At best they give only a partial, literally one-sided view of a building, and to ascertain its age you ought to be able to look all round it, and make yourself familiar with its locality and surroundings. When any forms or details are so well known as to be easily recognised, and their dates are known—as in the Gothic styles for instance—the case is different. Photographs at once tell all that is wanted to be known, and with perfect authenticity. But this is certainly not the case with Orissan temples as at present known. The thing will not be satisfactorily done till some one visits Orissa who has leisure, and at least a rudimentary knowledge of the principles of archæology. It would not require much, the buildings are so uniform in character, and their architects expressed so simply and unaffectedly the feelings and art of their age. Though despising archæology so thoroughly, the Babu cannot always escape its influence. At p. 71, for instance, he says: "One of them (a temple in the great temple enclosure), however, is worthy of note, as it is probably the oldest building in the courtyard, considerably older than even the great Tower." How did he ascertain this? There is no inscription, dated or otherwise; no tradition, not even a name. It must have been from some "preconceived theory." There must have been something in its style and appearance to have forced this very obvious fact on his attention, though he reprobates the admission of such evidence by others in unmeasured terms. There are, in fact, many among the seventy-eight temples in the enclosure which are certainly older than the great Temple, some of these are seen on plate xxx., but whether any of these is the one above alluded to by the Babu is not clear. He does not describe its locality with sufficient distinctness for its identification.

So far as can at present be made out, the key to the chronological arrangement of Orissan temples is to be found in the practical identity of style between the Mukteswara temples at Bhuvaneswara, and of the Black Pagoda at Konaruc. The one, it is true, is only a chapel, the other is a cathedral—to use the language of the Gothic styles—but if they are both in the "Decorated" or "Tudor" styles, that makes no difference to the archæologist. The next point is the certainty—I think absolute—that the Black Pagoda is a copy—a refined and improved one, of the great Temple at Bhuvaneswara, and that the distance in time between the two may be about a century. That, of course, is indeterminate to the extent of probably fifty years, more or less; every one must judge for himself. But the important historical fact which may very well be inferred from other circumstances is, that there were in the Kesari age two religious centres at Orissa. The first at

Bhuvaneswara, devoted wholly to the worship of Siva and the cognate cults. The other at Konaruc, which was the head-quarters of Vishnuism, Sun-worship, and similar manifestations of divine energy. There is no reason for supposing that the Vishnave religion was ever in abeyance during the Kesari dynasty, and, on the contrary, every reason for believing that its followers were at least equally numerous and as powerful as those of Siva; but, till the discovery of the date of the Konaruc temple, it was a mystery where they had hidden their pre-eminence from the eyes of the people. One great proof of this is that when, in 1132, the Chorganga dynasty succeeded the Kesari line, it transferred the focus of the Vishnave religion to Puri, and in 1200 it built the present temple there. It was after this the Vishnave religion assumed the first place, which it ever afterwards has retained in Orissa, but which could hardly have been the case if it had not possessed at least a nearly equal position under the previous dynasty.[1]

Without illustrations, and an amount of dissertation which is quite incompatible with a work like the present, it would be impossible to publish a list of Orissan temples, chronologically arranged, which would be of much value to outsiders. The main features of the classification are, as just explained, sufficiently obvious, and a tentative list may in the meanwhile be presented, as at least a foundation to enable others who have better opportunities, than I have, to complete it by filling in the *lacunæ*, and by correcting any mistakes that may have arisen from information depending mainly on photographic evidence and the impressions obtained from a very hurried visit to the place in 1837. At that time, however, my time was mainly occupied in making camera lucida sketches of the principal buildings, which I then thought of most importance, as those published before that time could not be depended upon for any archæological purpose. Three of them were afterwards published in my 'Picturesque Illustrations of Ancient Architecture in Hindostan,' and notwithstanding the absolute exactness since obtained by the introduction of photography, I have nothing to be ashamed of in them, considering that they

[1] Hunter's 'Orissa,' vol. i. p. 279.

passed, after leaving my sketch-book, through the hands of a lithographer entirely ignorant of style:—

YAYATI KESARI, founder of dynasty, 474 to 526 A.D.

First Group—

500 to 600.	Anonymous temple in great temple enclosure; 500? Sidesreswara—older than Kedereswara (p. 93). Kedereswara—said to be middle of sixth century (p. 93). Kapileswara—earlier than great temple (p. 96). Alabu Kesari?

Second Group—

600 to 750.	Moitre Serai—Sari Deül? Ananta Vasa Deva (p. 84) Bhoga Mandap, 1075? Great Temple 617–657, completed 667. Jomeswara—Someswara? Nakeswara. Baskereswara.

Third Group—

750 to 950.	Mukteswara. Great Temple at Konaruc—Black Pagoda. Gauri Devi. Brahmeswara. Markandeswara? (Puri, 811–829). Parasurameswara. Vaitala Deül (Kapila Devi). Rajarani.

FOUNDATION OF KATAK, 953–989.

Fourth Group—

950 to 1200.	Bhoga Mandap at Konaruc, now at Puri. Bhoga Mandap in Bhuvaneswara, 792–811. Nat Mandir in Bhuvaneswara, 1099–1104. Great Temple at Puri, 1175–1198.[1]

One of the greatest advantages to be derived from this, or any chronological classification of such a series of temples is, that it brings us nearer to a solution of one of the most obscure of the problems which still perplex the student of Indian architecture. For the last fifty years the question of the origin of the Hindu Sikhara has been constantly before my mind, and hundreds of solutions have from time to time suggested themselves, but all have been in turn rejected as insufficient to

[1] The figures in the above list are taken from the 'Antiquities of Orissa.'

account for the known phenomena. Though the one I am now about to propose looks more like a solution than any other that has occurred to me, it is far from being free from difficulties, and must at best be considered a mere hypothesis till some new facts are discovered which may either confirm or demolish it. The conclusion I have now arrived at is, that the Hindu Sikhara is derived from the Buddhist dagoba, or, in other words, is only a development of the style of architecture which was practised, both by Hindus and Buddhists, during the early ages in which stone architecture was practised, subsequent to the Mauryan epoch.

The idea is by no means a new or original one, and has been suggested by others as well as having frequently occurred to myself. Mr. Growse has, for instance, no doubt about the matter.[1] But as the examples from which he derived his conviction extend no further back than the temple of Parsanath, at Khajaraho, of the eleventh century, and he only traces it from that through the singularly abnormal temples at Bindrabun, his reasoning cannot be relied upon, though his conclusion may accidentally be right. The Orissan series carries us back at least five centuries nearer to the point of divergence, and offers examples presenting features having much more affinity to Buddhist architecture than these very late examples. Even then, however, it requires a very considerable familiarity with the subject in all its bearings, and it may be added a considerable faculty of imagination, to see the connection between two such apparently dissimilar objects. Take, for instance, a typical example of a Buddhist stupa, such, for instance, as the tope at Sanchi, and place it beside a typical example of a Hindu temple such as the great one at Bhuvaneswara, and it seems at first sight impossible to trace any connection between them. Yet I am convinced it did exist, and can be traced, when sufficient attention is paid to its essential peculiarities.

The great difficulty of proving the connection lies in a peculiarity of the case which it is difficult for even those most

[1] 'Mathura, a district Memoir.' By F. S. Growse. Second edition, published by Government. Quarto, 1880, p. 236.

familiar with history of Indian architecture fully to realise. It is this: though we have an almost unlimited number of examples of cave architecture between the reigns of Asoka, 250 B.C. and of Yayati Kesari, 500 A.D.—some, it is true, mere copies of wooden architecture, but gradually hardening into lithic forms, and at last becoming a purely masonic architecture of stone—still, during the whole of these seven centuries and a half, we have not one single exterior of a building, either in wood or stone. Among the earliest exteriors we possess are the Raths at Mahavellipur (A.D. 750), and about them there is no difficulty; they are almost literal copies of the viharas, chaityas, and halls of the Buddhists—conventionalised, of course, to suit the requirements of a religion different from, almost antagonistic in fact to that for which the originals were designed, but still preserving its peculiarities so completely that every feature can be easily recognised. The people in the south adopted them as models, and all the features of the Dravidian style were copied from them, and remain traceable back to the original—down even to the present day—so that with regard to the Dravidian architecture there is no difficulty. Its derivation from the Buddhist architecture of the early ages of Christianity is evident, even on the most cursory examination, and has never been disputed. With the northern styles, however, the case is widely different. But are we justified in assuming that all the viharas of the Buddhists had pyramidal roofs formed in terraces and adorned with cells like the Dharmaraja Ratha [1] at Mahavellipur? Is it not possible that some at least of them had roofs formed of wooden or bambu framing, and covered with thatch or metal like the Draupadi Ratha at the same place.[2]

The assumption of the thatched or metal-covered roof gets over half at least of the difficulty, as it gets rid of the necessity for the horizontal lines which is so marked a characteristic of the Dravidian as compared with the northern style, and also accounts—assuming bambus to be used, from the curved outline which otherwise seems so puzzling. Some such form of

[1] 'Cave Temples of India,' p. 124, woodcut 32.

[2] Loc. cit., p. 116, woodcut 27.

roof seems a necessity of the case, for the Indians at that time do not seem to have been able to form the flat-terraced roofs so common in Persia, and generally in Central Asia. In none of the bas-reliefs of the Sanchi tope or the earlier examples, are flat-roofed houses represented, and it may therefore be assumed

No. 8.—Dagoba in Cave 19, at Ajunta. 550 A.D. ?
(From a sketch by the Author.)

that none such existed, and this may account for the form of the upright part of the tower. It does not, however, account for the dome-like termination, called the Amla sila or ribbed moulding, which is so essential and so characteristic. The usual theory that this last feature is copied from the Amalki or Amalaki fruit (*Phyllanthus emblica*) is too fanciful and far-fetched to be worthy of consideration, but I think it may fairly be considered as representing the chattni, or umbrella, that universally crowns the dagobas of the Buddhists. If we take, for instance, the accompanying representation of the dagoba in Cave 19 at Ajunta, we see that what was originally a very simple and mound-like form of a stupa has grown into a tall form not very unlike a Hindu temple, and supposing it was crowned by only one chatta instead of three, and the ridge of that one was ribbed,[1] we would get very near what we are

No. 9.—Ribbed Capital from Elephanta.

looking for. It does not seem an unlikely supposition that ribbing may have been so employed, at a very early time, as ribbed capitals were so employed in the earliest caves, and continued to be so used till they were perfected, at Elephanta and Elura, as shown in this form. In all the earlier temples,

[1] By accident the umbrellas in this sketch are represented as ribbed, which is not the case. The appearance when I made the sketch must have arisen from bats' dung or weather stains. The place is very dark, so dark indeed, that no photograph that I have shows its details with sufficient distinctness to engrave from it a correct representation.

both in the west and east, ribbed angle-pieces were inserted after every third and fourth course, and frequently with a band round them, as shown in the last woodcut, and as it occurs in the very oldest temples in Orissa. The most essential difference between the two styles in these earlier stages, is that the tendency of all the decorative lines in the Buddhist architecture is towards the horizontal, while in the Hindu it is as generally towards the vertical, and the difficulty is very great in reconciling these two opposite tendencies in styles supposed to have a common origin. When, however, we take into account the immense gap that occurs—five or six centuries—between what we may assume as the origin of the Hindu style, and its first known example, it is evident that we must be content with slightest indications of affinity, and the vaguest surmises of its common origin with the Buddhist style. I am not, however, without hopes that by patient investigation even these may before long assume a position of considerable certainty among the acknowledged facts of Indian archæology.

If the relevance of these remarks is admitted even in a modified degree, it probably will appear to most people, when examining such a temple as that represented in the annexed wood-

No. 10.—Upper part of a Temple at Bhuvaneswara. (From a Photograph.)

cut, that there can be very little doubt that it is taken from the same original as the later Buddhist dagobas. It represents one of the oldest of the temples in the enclosure of the great temple at Bhuvaneswara, not probably the very oldest, but certainly very long anterior to the great temple. If we assume the dome with its ribbed moulding and four supporting figures like those in Cave 19 at Ajunta, which are of about the same age, to represent the chattri, we have a reasonable suggestion for its appearance, and as the angles of the tower itself are bevelled off, it assumes, like many of the earliest temples, a nearly rounded form in plan, which does not occur in more modern temples. In these the four angles are always more strongly marked, which, so far as it goes, is an argument for the earlier examples being derived from a circular original.

On the whole, the evidence, such as we possess, seems to show that at some early period—say about the Christian era—India possessed only one style of external architecture, and that was in the possession of the Buddhists; but in the next five centuries—during which we know nothing of their architecture—the Hindus selected portions of the style and adapted them to their own purposes, and so elaborated the complete style which bursts upon us in the reign of the early kings of the Kesari dynasty. A little reflection on the part of any one familiar with the facts of the case, will show how difficult and perplexing the problem is, as presented to us. If we assume that only one style of architecture prevailed in India in the age of Asoka (B.C. 250), or at any given period before or after that, we know perfectly well, from the caves, what the Buddhists did and were aiming at in their dagobas, and in the interiors of their chaitya halls and viharas. We have examples by hundreds during the next ten centuries. But the exteriors being at least principally, if not wholly, in wood, have all perished without a single exception. What consequently the external appearance of these buildings was—except the stupas—we learn, for the first time, from the raths at Mahavellipur (A.D. 750). The Hindus were at the same time, we may assume, using the same architectural elements, but for a totally different purpose. Their object was to elaborate a temple of a dignified exterior, irrespective of internal use or ornament. It is consequently no wonder that when the first example is presented to us in Orissa, about A.D. 500, it should be so divergent from the exteriors of the Buddhists, that we are hardly able to recognise that they spring from the same originals. We have no examples, either in wood or stone, from which we can follow the steps by which the divergence took place, or by which, to use the language of naturalists, the variety assumed the fixed character of a species, and this—to follow out the same simile—is aggravated by our ignorance of the form and character of the parent style from which they both sprung.

The Hindu being essentially a stone architecture, it is just possible that some examples earlier than A.D. 500 may yet be discovered, and if they are, they will do more to throw light on the history of the devèlopment of the Hindu form of religion than anything derived from any other source.

CHAPTER IV.

BUDDHA GAYA AND BRINDABUN.

The controversy with regard to the age of the temple at Buddha Gaya, which for some time past has ruffled the surface of the puddle of Indian archæology, has been brought to a sudden, though very unsatisfactory termination by the restorations executed by Mr. Beglar under General Cunningham's directions. After the discovery of the rail and other features of Asoka's time by Major Mead, in 1864, it was natural that the General should wish to clear away all the rubbish which encumbered the terrace of the temple. In doing so he made some very interesting discoveries, but there was no occasion why he should immediately undertake a restoration, which nearly amounts to a rebuilding of the whole, and has practically obliterated almost all the ancient features. A building which has stood, at all events, for 500 years, without showing any symptoms of cracks, or shakes, that would in the least endanger its stability, might very well have waited a year or two, till some architect, or other qualified person, could be procured from England, or elsewhere, to make careful drawings of the building and of its details before undertaking its restoration. The General himself is no architect, and does not pretend to be one. Except as a copy of a photograph the only attempt at an architectural representation that appears in any one of his sixteen volumes of Reports, is that of the temple of Sidnath, near Kangra Kote (vol. v., plate xliv.), and it is so unlike the original, I defy any one to recognise it as a representation of this temple, without the inscription on the plate to say so.[1] Nowhere else does he attempt to show that he can make an architectural section or elevation of a building; and his assistant Mr. Beglar is even less accomplished in this respect than his master. The few attempts at drawing architectural details that are dispersed through his reports are more like the production of a half-educated schoolboy than anything that would be thought worthy of publication by a full-grown man.

The truth of the matter seems to be that General Cunningham chooses his assistants, not because of their fitness for the work they have to perform, but rather because of their incompetence, in order that they may not forestall the credit he thinks may accrue to him, from the great work he one day hopes to be able to publish on Indian archæology. He seems to be afraid that some one should appropriate to himself a share of what he thinks belongs to him, and him only. On any other theory, at least, it seems impossible to account for his employment during so many years of so incompetent an assistant as Mr. Carlleyle. During the fourteen years he has been employed on the survey, he has contributed almost literally nothing to our knowledge of archæology or architectural geography. His last great effort to settle the site of Kapilavastu (Report xii.) is one of the most unsatisfactory essays of its sort that can well be conceived. It may be at Bhuila, as General Cunningham thinks, but the evidence that it is so is of the most unconvincing nature, and will not stand a moment's investigation. My own impression is that it was considerably more to the southward. Mr. Beglar is a much better man, and there is a considerable amount of earnestness and independence[2] about him; and though he has not the accomplishments that would qualify him for his post, he has done some good work, and under proper guidance might have done more.

[1] There is a representation of this temple from a photograph in my 'History of Indian Architecture,' p. 316, woodcut 178, which will afford a means of comparison.

[2] His investigation of the Sattapani Cave question, in opposition to the views expressed by General Cunningham, vol. viii. p. 89, shows considerable acumen and power of investigation. See 'Cave Temples of India,' p. 49.

Before commencing his works of restoration at Buddha Gaya, Mr. Beglar wrote to me on 26th January, 1880, asking my advice regarding them, and enclosing me a copy of a memorandum he had addressed to the General, explaining in detail what he proposed. I have not kept a copy of my reply, but it was to this effect: "For heaven's sake, don't! Fill up all cranks with cement, cover the roof with either asphalte or cement to prevent infiltration. If buttresses or arches are necessary to maintain the fabric, build them with modern bricks, and in modern forms, so that they may not possibly be mistaken for ancient work. In short, do anything that may be necessary to maintain the fabric; but restore nothing, and, above all, destroy no feature, however insignificant it may appear; you cannot know of what value it may be eventually." This was at least the substance of my advice, but its form was of the least possible consequence, as a directly opposite course was pursued.

According to Major Mead, who first disclosed the form of the terrace on which the temple stands, "The southern basement of the temple was first exposed, which is singularly perfect and handsome, although entirely in plaster."[1] It has now been entirely rebuilt in brickwork, according to a design by Mr. Beglar. The northern face of the terrace had been rebuilt in plain brickwork long ago, either by the Burmese or some one else. The western face was untouched, and very interesting when my last photograph was taken, and if left alone would stand for a hundred years at least. I do not know whether Mr. Beglar has carried out his intention of roofing over the porch on the east face, according to a design of his own, which is as unlike what the original may be supposed to have been as can well be imagined. The recasing of the tower on the west face was only carried to about half its height when my last photographs were taken; but, from what I hear, it is probably complete. The temple of Tara Devi, which certainly required no repairs, is now made "as good as new," and as hideous as a modern restorer could desire. The

[1] 'Buddha Gaya,' p. 63.

expense of these restorations, according to Major Cole,[1] has been about R.80,000, while 8000 would certainly have sufficed for all that was wanted to conserve the building, and maintain it in a sufficient state of repair to last for many years to come. The larger sum was only required to obliterate as far as possible every ancient feature.

If General Cunningham has preserved a sufficient number of photographs of the temple, in its various stages during the renovation, and will even now employ a competent architect to make measurements and drawings of what still remains, the damage done may to a certain extent be repaired. He has the materials from which a most interesting monograph may be written, and from which all the main facts of its history may be obtained. The poetry and beauty of the building is gone for ever, but there may still be a good deal of prosaic information to be extracted from it, which will no doubt prove interesting to the history of Buddhism, and may aid in enabling us to trace the progress of architecture in Central India.[2]

Whatever may be thought of the policy of this restoration, there is no doubt that the excavations that preceded it have furnished materials from which the history of the monument can be ascertained with far greater exactness than was previously the case. The discovery of the Vajrasana, or diamond throne of Asoka, on the same level as the rail, which is almost certainly of his age, and the knowledge that he did erect a vihara on the spot where the present temple stands, give us a firm foundation from which to reason as to the age of the building. But the interval that elapses before we get any further authentic information regarding it, is practically enormous. It was nine hundred years after Asoka's

[1] 'First Report of the Conservator of Ancient Monuments in India,' 1882, p. 43.

[2] From a paragraph in the preface of his last Report, vol. xvi., I see he proposes such a publication under the title of 'Mahabodhi,' in conjunction with Mr. Beglar. If satisfactorily accomplished, it will go far to atone for his destruction of the building; but unless they can associate an architect with them, or some one who can draw architectural details, the work will, I fear, be a failure.

time that Hiouen Thsang visited the spot, and left a description of it, the correctness of which we have no reason to doubt, and which forms the second epoch in its history. The tree and all the buildings of Asoka were in all probability originally on the same level, but successive mounds raised on the planting of successive trees during this long interval had accumulated the earth to a height of 20 to 25 feet, so that the floor of the cella of the temple, which he saw, was raised to that level, or nearly so when he visited the place.

It is not easy to fix with any precision the date of the erection of the temple which Hiouen Thsang saw and described. It certainly did not exist when Fa Hian visited the place (A.D. 400), but if there is any reliance to be placed on the Amara Sinha inscription,[1] it may have been erected 100 years after that time, say about 500, which is the date General Cunningham assumes,[2] and I believe correctly. If this is so, the investigations we have above been attempting into the forms and histories of Orissan temples bring us at once into contact with contemporary examples, which enable us to understand Hiouen Thsang's description without difficulty. The porch, which he says was afterwards added to it, with its three doors and its triple roof, is a counterpart of the porch of the temple at Konaruc (the Black Pagoda). If we can carry back the design of that temple for a century and a half or two centuries, which with existing examples is not difficult, we have the porch at Buddha Gaya exactly reproduced. The one essential feature in which they differed is that the porch at Buddha Gaya was two storeys in height, but that arose from the circumstance that the floor of the temple had been raised 20 or 25 feet, from the accumulations of earth to accommodate the trees, and consequently a lower storey was

[1] Translated by Wilkins in the first volume of the 'Asiatic Researches.' Babu Rajendralala in the 'Buddha Gaya' attempts to prove (p. 201 *et seq.*) that it is a forgery, and unworthy of any consideration. It appears to me, however, on very insufficient ground, and by very inconclusive reasoning. It is, however, of the least possible consequence for the history of the building whether this is so or not. If it is a forgery, the building *may* be 50 years more modern. It could hardly be 100, under any circumstance.

[2] Reports, vol. i. p. 8.

indispensable. Whether the tower was exactly like that represented in woodcut No. 10 is not quite so clear. The temple represented in the woodcut is of about the same age—about 500 A.D.—and in the same style, and probably, *mutatis mutandis*, resembled it in all essential respects. It would of course be extremely interesting to trace these similarities, were this the place to do it. But every step in that direction tends to strengthen the argument that the building which now exists at Buddha Gaya is not the one that Hiouen Thsang saw. It was a building of blue bricks, and all its features were expressed in brickwork. The present building, though constructed with bricks, is coated from basement to the kalasa with a thick covering of stucco, and all its architectural features and ornaments, and all its sculptures, are executed in that material. This alone is sufficient to prove that the present building is most essentially different from the building he saw, and consequently any attempt to investigate its peculiarities would be entirely out of place.

We have nothing but architectural evidence to enable us to fix the period when the first stucco-coated edifice was erected; but, from such materials as are now available, I should have very little hesitation in fixing the year 1000 A.D. as a medium date. It may be 100 years earlier, or a like number later, but as a mean this cannot, it seems to me, be far wrong. It is almost impossible that Hiouen Thsang's temple could have escaped destruction during the dark period of Buddhist persecution that elapsed from 700 to 900. During these two centuries Buddhists, or at least Buddhist buildings, entirely disappear from India.[1] In the west they never reappeared, but in Bengal there was a Buddhist revival, under the Pala dynasty. Under them the temple at Buddha Gaya seems to have been rebuilt and decorated in a very beautiful style. From other examples of that age with which we are tolerably familiar we know what this style really was; and this terrace now remains so, or did till the period of Mr. Beglar's restoration, a very beautiful specimen of its class.

[1] 'History of Indian Architecture,' pp. 24–209. 'Cave Temples of India,' p. 397.

We have no means of knowing what the state of the tower was in the eleventh century, when the terrace was rebuilt. It is of brick, set in mud, evidently of no great antiquity, and depending almost wholly, even for its existence, on its thick coating of stucco in which all its architectural and sculptural features are expressed. These are of a very different and certainly more modern form than those of the terrace, and may have been added by the Burmese or by any one else during the three centuries that elapsed from the time of the rebuilding of the terrace till the Muhammadan invasion.

For myself, I see no reason for doubting the statements made in the famous Burmese inscription under the date of 1305, which ascribes the last rebuilding or recasing to the king of Arakan of that day.[1] Now that we know so much of the real history of the building, it is hardly worth quarrelling about. From the inscription it seems the Burmese must have been perfectly familiar with its history. The vihara of Asoka having fallen into decay, it was rebuilt by Naikmahanta (in 500 A.D. ?); having again been ruined, it was rebuilt by Sado Mung (A.D. 1000 ?); and again having been destroyed or fallen into decay, it was rebuilt by the Guru Raja Guna, who, after various delays, completed this third restoration in 1305, and gave it the appearance it wore till 1880, when a fourth repair or recasing was undertaken by Mr. Beglar under General Cunningham's auspices, with what result remains to be seen.

If any further information is to be obtained regarding the history of this most interesting temple, it is only by a careful study of what remains of it by some one not only familiar with the artistic peculiarities of Indian styles, but also of the constructive modes employed by their builders. It will be extremely difficult to find any one equal to the task, and if he were found, it would be hardly worth while now to undertake it. The building has lost much of the interest that once attached to it, and much of the mystery that once hung about its origin has already been dispelled. It is scarcely probable that any traces will now be found of the temple erected in 500 A.D.; and having the basement of the temple which succeeded it

[1] 'Buddha Gaya,' p. 206–208.

in or about 1000, we are not now so anxious about it; while to the Burmese restoration that followed we can refer to the Bodhi temple at Paghan, which was erected about the year 1200, and is in every respect as exact a copy of what the Buddha Gaya temple was at that time as it is possible to find in a non-copying age. Though erected for the same purpose—the honour of the Bo tree—and meant no doubt to be an exact reproduction of its prototype, the architects of that age did not, and could not, confine themselves to mere copying, but reproduced the temple with such improvement and alteration as their fancy dictated, and as the customs of the building fraternity on the banks of the Irrawady suggested.[1] It is, however, marvellously like the Buddha Gaya temple, and well worthy of the attentive study of those who are interested in the appearance of that temple as refaced by the Burmese in 1305. I possess photographs of it, which render the affinities between the two temples even more clear than any engravings could do.[2]

Under the circumstances just described, it would have been a great gain if in 1877 the Government of Bengal had been able to

[1] Crawfurd's 'Embassy to Ava,' octavo edition, vol. i. p. 116.

[2] The presence of brick-lining arches in the tower, if they still exist, has long ceased to be of any chronological importance. I have already stated ('Cave Temples of India,' p. 133) what effect recent investigations have had on the subject. From the fact that the Burmese used brick arches, in every form, at Paghan between the 10th and 13th centuries, and owing to the constant communications at that time, it is no wonder that they might have been used in any brick building of the Pala age, as well as afterwards. Some may even have been found as internal linings in brick temples at even an earlier age, but nothing has yet been discovered that would lead us to suppose that they were employed even for this subordinate purpose earlier than the sixth or seventh century, and never even then for external or constructive purposes, till a much later period. If the Sonbhandar Cave could be shown to be identical with the Sattapanni Cave, in which the first convocation was held, it would make the Babu's contention even more absurd than it is (p. 109). It has, however, been sufficiently proved that this is not the case ('Cave Temples,' p. 49), but as it must be at least one or two centuries B.C., no one but the Babu would suppose its roof represented an arch—nor would he, except for the sake of contradicting me, on the principle that whatever I say must be wrong and ought "*per fas aut nefas*" to be contradicted.

find some one who, either by his accomplishments as an artist or of his knowledge as an archæologist, could have been deputed to write a report on this temple before its restoration was undertaken. As money was no object, and they were prepared to place all the resources of their typographical and artistic establishments at the disposal of their envoy, he might easily have produced a monograph that would have left nothing to be desired. With 50 quarto plates and 250 quarto pages of text, all the artistic peculiarities of the temple might have been illustrated to the fullest desirable extent, and the history of the building elucidated as far as the materials available would admit of its being done. Unfortunately, no such person appears to have existed, or at least none was found in Calcutta, and in an evil moment the mission was entrusted to Babu Rajendralala, and the consequence is the production of a work which adds nothing to our previous knowledge of the appearance of the building, and which it is no exaggeration to say does not contribute one new fact to our knowledge of its history, nor to the elucidation of the many problems of Indian archæology which it pretends to treat of with such redundant learning.[1]

He begins his illustrations, of a certain class, by copying two plans of the temple made by General Cunningham (pl. iv.). Why these are reproduced is by no means apparent, as they do not illustrate any proposition in the text, and they are so drawn here as to be very little use unless it is to show how worthless is his own plan of the building. Being in different works, and drawn for different purposes, they are not to the same scale, but, as is his wont, the General was careful to add elaborate scales to each plate. If the Babu had reproduced them to the same scale, they might have been useful for comparison; but this he has not attempted, but has drawn them, not only to the different dimensions adopted by the General, but to a scale different from his, in both instances; and, as he carefully omits the scales from his plates, the plans are absolutely useless for any intelligible purpose. The only motive that occurs to me that could have

[1] 'Buddha Gaya. The hermitage of Sakya Muni.' By Rajendralala Mitra, LL.D., C.I.E., &c. Calcutta, 1878.

induced the Babu to reproduce these plans—besides filling a plate—seems to have been the idea that he could produce a better, and this he proceeds to do in the next plate (pl. v.), which is certainly unique in plan-drawing.

There is no scale, of course: the Babu despises such matter-of-fact devices; but, after considerable difficulties, I guess that it is meant to be 50 feet to 1 inch, because there is a measurement 97 feet 10 inches, measured from the temple to the enclosure, which exactly fits this scale. Applying it consequently to the other nine dimensions which he has figured on the plan, we have the following results:—

1.	97·10 correct on scale of 50 feet to 1 inch.				
2.	212·6	scales	225·0	difference	8·6
3.	236·0	„	240·0	„	4·0
4.	75·6	„	50·0	„	25·6
5.	48·0	„	57·6	„	9·6
6.	26·0	„	50·0	„	24·0
7.	34·4	„	40·0	„	5·8
8.	42·3	„	75·0	„	22·9
9.	10·4	„	15·0	„	4.8

Some of these differences it would not be necessary to remark upon if they stood alone, but the whole make up an amount of errors that it would not be easy to match on any plan in modern times.

It is not only, however, in his dimensions that the Babu goes astray. The plan of the temple is hatched in a manner that, according to the usual principles of plan-drawing, is quite incomprehensible. If it is a section through the terrace, which, in one sense, it pretends to be, the tree and its encircling masonry ought not to be shown, still less the cella, which is certainly not in the basement. If it is a section through the tower, the cella is right, but the tree wrong; but what the apartment C means, and what the angles K K, nor how the stairs in front at I and D are arranged, it is difficult to understand. The fact is, the Babu or his assistant have attempted to represent on one plane the temple at two different heights. Plan-drawers in this country, where it is necessary to do this, draw a broken or crooked line through their pictures, and represent one half in section the other in plan, on the different sides of this line. The Babu was probably not aware of this device, and consequently, drawing a plan according to his own unaided light, has made the unintelligible muddle shown in plate v.

Unfortunately, the shortcomings of the Babu's book are not confined to the plans. On plate viii. he exhibits a restored elevation of the building, which, without being absolutely incorrect, so far as he affords means of judging, is as unlike the existing building as it can possibly be. So little conscious is he of this defect, that in plate vii. he prints a photograph, which challenges comparison with the restoration. Very considerable allowances must of course be made for the foreshortening of the latter, as affecting the proportions of the outline, but it does not alter the character of the details or their relative proportions *inter se*, which give so totally different appearance to the building. Avowedly his artist has introduced one storey too many, but this is trivial in comparison to his missing and misrepresenting the whole character of the details. The thickening the stem of the tree by at least one-third alters the whole character of this feature of the building,[1] and the immense exaggeration of that part of the building, in the restoration, throws the design of the whole out of proportion to an almost inconceivable extent. But what could we expect? A geometric elevation of a building made avowedly without measurement, and published without a scale, is not likely to represent its features correctly, and is an experiment in architectural drawing which we hope will not be often repeated.

In support of his views of the Buddha Gaya temple, and his restoration of it, the Babu introduces a photograph of the temple at Konch (plate xviii.). He professes to see the most marked similarity of design and affinity between the two

[1] At page 81. The Babu objects to my assertion that the number of rings in the Kalasa never exceed 9. I do not yet know of any *structural* example in which that number is surpassed. In small models of single stones, I of course know that they are found with any number of rings up to 50. But these are not buildings, and of those alone I was speaking.

temples; while I, on the contrary, see none. In fact, it is my inability to perceive this that so long made me hesitate to ascribe a common origin to the Hindu and Buddhist styles, but which, as just explained above, I am now inclined to admit. The characteristic, it appears to me, of the Buddha Gaya tower, is the marked division into storeys, and the consequently horizontal lines of ornamentation that prevail throughout. In the Konch tower there is not a shadow of a reminiscence of a storeyed form, and all the lines of decoration are vertical. The mode of reconciling these opposite systems that now occurs to me is that the Buddha Gaya style is derived from the vihara, the Konch from the dagoba. The two forms apparently deviated from one another at some very early age. The Buddhists retaining the one, in a very modified form, it must be confessed, down at least to the time of the Buddha Gaya temple; the Hindus appropriating the other, and elaborating out of it, with modifications suggested by the vihara form, the style we now find in Orissa and at Konch. The more I think of it, the more probable does it appear that this is the true solution of the problem, and it may at least be adopted as a true hypothesis, till at least some better is suggested.

Besides the value in the Babu's eyes, of the temple at Konch, as illustrating the architecture of that at Buddha Gaya, it occurred to him that it might be useful in refuting my heresies about the arch; he therefore published on page 78 a woodcut section, of which that on the following page is a facsimile. It will at first be observed, on comparing it with the photograph (plate xviii.), that the outline of the sikhara is quite different; but that is of comparatively little importance; but above the doorway he has introduced a triangular opening, or window, 15 feet high by about 7½ feet wide, which *does not exist*. It is a curious illustration of how uneducated his eye is, that with the photograph staring him in the face, he does not perceive the impossibility of an opening as he represents in the woodcut, existing where he places it. The fact of the matter is, that nine-tenths of the difficulties and discrepancies that occur, both in this book and in the 'Antiquities of Orissa,' arise from the total want of education of the eye, which is everywhere apparent. This arises apparently from his never learning to draw in his youth, or never at least practising it in his mature age, which was a fatal deficiency

No. 11.—Section of Temple at Konch. (From 'Buddha Gaya,' p. 78.)

when he undertook to enlighten the world on matters of art and archæology.

I hope I may be spared saying many words about the Babu's design for the triple front of the temple on plate xix. It is not quite clear whether he intends it to be a restored representation of the temple, as it was seen by Hiouen Thsang (640 A.D.), or whether it represents it as rebuilt by the Palas (A.D. 1000), or as it was left by the Burmese in 1305. Whichever is intended, we may safely say that nothing so hideous and unsuitable was ever erected by any Indian architect, or even proposed, anterior to the nineteenth century. Mr. Beglar seems in 1880 to have been perfectly aware of its unsuitableness—to say the least of it—and consequently is not likely to have made any attempt to reproduce it; and as the Babu's patrons are no longer in power in Calcutta, there is little more harm likely to come of it than the production of an autotype plate, which will hurt no one but its designer.

The selection and the arrangement of the sculptures depicted in the 12 plates, xx. to xxxii., is marked by that want of method and total want of power to discriminate styles, which characterises all that Babu Rajendralala does. From the conventional mode in which plates xxiv. and xxx. are drawn, and the absence of any emblems they may be of any age. My conviction is that they are not earlier than the others. Among these there is certainly not one that is earlier than the Pala age, tenth to twelfth century, and many are very much more modern. Some are Burmese, some are modern Hindu, and the bulk of them would be more appropriate to illustrate a work on the Black Pagoda at Calcutta, that one understood to be devoted to "Hermitage of Sakya Muni." The fifteen plates xxxiii. to xlvii. are among the most valuable in the work, and if we could depend on the drawing, would be a valuable contribution to our knowledge of the style of sculpture and decoration adopted in the Mauryan era, either by Asoka or his immediate successors. They have been already drawn by General Cunningham in the first volume of his Reports, pls. viii. to xi., not so completely, nor perhaps in some respects so well. But the best set of copies were made by Captain Kittoe, and are now in the library of the India Office, but still unpublished. They are, however, sufficient to show how imperfect the two other copies are, and how indispensable it is that they should be reproduced by photography. It seems almost impossible to eliminate the personal equation, and when we are dealing with such archaic and unfamiliar forms, nothing but a mechanical process will suffice. General Cunningham's copy of the gate pillar, photographed on plate l., is sufficient to show how indispensable this is.[1] It is impossible to reason from any such drawings as have hitherto been produced. Plate xlviii. is a curious specimen of how things are huddled together in this work. Fig. 1 is a corner pillar of the Asoka rail, with an inscription in the Lât character, and ought therefore to have been classed and described with them. Fig. 2 is a pillar from the so-called vihara of Baladitya at Nalanda, excavated and figured by Broadley, though how it got to Calcutta is by no means clear. The lintel, fig. 3, is also from the same excavation, and is particularly interesting here as possessing on the outer edge the same foliated moulding that we remarked on in page 61, woodcut, No. 7, as occurring in the Mukteswara temple and the Black Pagoda, and elsewhere. It is here represented probably in a slightly more modern form, but the lintel to which it is attached cannot possibly be later than the ninth or tenth century, and may be earlier, possibly as early as the eighth.

Plates x., xi., and xii. seem to have got singularly astray in the arrangements of the plates, and even more so in their description in the text, yet they are among the most interesting, and, for the history of the building, the most important plates in the book. They are, from their style and details, evidently of the same age, and one of them has an inscription (pl. xi.), dated from the form of its characters. It is amusing, however, to see how easily the "sober-minded" Babu puts a dated inscription on one side when it does not suit his "preconceived theories" that it should be adopted. Anyone at all familiar with the character of sculpture in Behar in the tenth century would recognise the figure of Buddha with the emblems beneath it as belonging to the tenth or eleventh century, and it hardly needed the Kutila inscription on its base to confirm it (page 133). If it is of that age, the Buddha depicted plate x. is so also, and that fixes the age of the whole terrace of the building. Though not so evident at first sight—from the imperfection of the drawing—the three groups B C and D on plate xii. are evidently of the same age. The architecture of

[1] If I am rightly informed, the photograph on plate l. is taken from a cast in the Calcutta Museum, not from the original sculpture. See 'Anderson's Catalogue,' p. 124.

the niches in which they stand and their whole appearance confirms this. It is true the facile pencil of the Babu's artist, Bagchi, has a wonderful tendency to reduce all Hindu sculpture to a common denomination, which makes the demand for photographs more imperative; but, though from the drawing here given it might be difficult to date these sculptures within a century or two, to take them back to Asoka's time, B.C. 250, is rather too strong. If he had contended that they belonged to the temple of Amara (the one Hiouen Thsang saw), he might have convinced some people. But the changes in the character of Indian sculpture were too great and too rapid, as we know from our experience at Sanchi and Amaravati, for any one to be deceived, when the two extremities of these tenth and twelfth centuries are fairly presented to him. They are certainly not of Asoka's time, nor even of Amara's, but almost certainly belong to the Pala restoration of the temple. In fact we have not yet found any vestige either of sculpture or architecture which can be ascribed to the time of the earlier temple.[1] The throne, plate xii. fig. A, so far as can be made out from the drawing, seems certainly to belong to that age. It may be that some further researches may bring to light some vestiges of the temple which Hiouen Thsang saw and described, but certainly none yet have been discovered. How far any parts of its structure may be encased and hidden in the present temple is, of course, impossible to say, but nothing certainly is to be seen outside.

It would be tedious, as it certainly would be unprofitable, to attempt to answer all the arguments the Babu adduces against my theories. The process would interest no one but myself, and I can very well afford to pass it over in silence. In nine cases out of ten the mode of argument adopted is by first misrepresenting the statements made by me, and then refuting his own misstatements, which is an easy enough process. If people read the Babu's books instead of mine, to learn my opinion on any subject, they will learn much that is curious

[1] Of course this remark does not apply to Vajrasana and the rail of Asoka—these can hardly be called parts of the temple.

and novel, but which it never entered into my head to propound, nor for which, if I am right, the public will not be either wiser or better. There is one argument, however, which is an exception to the general rule, and as it is stated fairly enough, deserves notice, though I differ entirely from his conclusions.

From a long and attentive study of the early rails of the Buddhists, I arrived at the conclusion that they were almost literal copies of some form of wooden construction. All their decorative and constructive features seem to point so conclusively to this, that I cannot even now understand how any one now can fancy that they were derived from forms of stone construction, or by a people using stone for building purposes. I do not quite understand that even the Babu adopts any such theory. He is of opinion, however, that "against animals a much lighter structure would have amply sufficed for protection" (p. 148), or "to save a small tree from the attacks of cattle" (p. 151), all which may be perfectly true, but misses the whole point of the argument. Very much lighter rails than those copied by the Buddhists in stone would have amply sufficed for agricultural purposes; but this suggestion does not attempt any explanation as to how these agricultural rails grew into those massive forms which we know from manifold experience were afterwards raised in stone, copied from wooden originals.

The Babu sneers at what he calls my "nail-headed" theory (page 150). Perhaps I may be mistaken. It is merely a suggestion to account for peculiarities which to me are inexplicable. I found that bronze discs and clamps were used in Greece to accentuate and adorn wooden constructions,[1] and it appeared to me that it might be so used in India. I cannot otherwise account for the form of the discs and half discs which ornamented the rails. Otherwise what are they? They are not reminiscences of either wooden or stone construction, and, as suggested above, it occurred to me that they must consequently be copied from forms in metal, probably bronze. But has the Babu any other theory to suggest? If not, mere fault-finding, though very gratifying to some minds, is very unprofitable.

[1] 'Parthenon,' p. 114.

The following paragraph, when treating of this subject, is a fair specimen of the Babu's mode of reporting my opinions as facts :—

"These changes could not have taken place within the single reign of A'soka; and yet, if we are to believe Mr. Fergusson, the art of sculpture was first originated in his reign, and the rails and stone-houses were for the first time made in stone from wooden models, and as the rails were put up by A'soka, the change was accomplished in fifteen to thirty years. Admitting, however, for the sake of argument, what is otherwise quite inadmissible, that the beginning and progress of stone rail-making was accomplished in the single reign of A'soka, it might be asked—How does this accord with the other theories of the learned author, in which he attributes the beginning of stone masonry and sculpture to the advent of Greek artists in India during A'soka's reign?[1] If accomplished artists came from Greece or Bactria, why did they begin by copying wooden models, and not introduce a completed art? Why should they have preferred lens-shaped tenons and mortices, which were not common in Greece or Bactria, to square and round ones, with which they were perfectly

[1] In 1865, when writing about the architecture of Persia I used an expression more definite than I would have used in writing about the architecture of India, where the context would have qualified my meaning. I meant to emphasise the proposition that the Assyrians and Persians had not employed stone for architectural purposes, till they came into contact with the Egyptians and Greeks and other stone-using people.—I added "the Indians first learned this *art* from the Bactrian Greeks." The word *art*, it must be confessed, is too indefinite. I ought, and would, if I had dreamt of the use that would be made of it, have qualified it by "architecture, as contra-distinguished from building or engineering," but I did not then think that such amplifications were necessary or desirable. At p. 50 of his 'Indo-Aryans,' Babu Rajendra prints this paragraph in capitals, as triumphantly proving his contention; and as he gives a reference only to an old edition of my general history, which has long been out of print, it is almost impossible that any one should find the passage, or see the bearing of the context. In fact, the Babu's mode of arguing the question would be thought ingenious and creditable in a lawyer trying to obtain a conviction for some high crime or misdemeanour at the Old Bailey. It has not, however, yet been introduced, so far as I know, into disputes regarding questions of science or art, and I hope never may be.

familiar? Doubtless the number of the artists who came from beyond India was not large, and they had to train up the natives of the country to practise the art; but, in such a case, the pupils, whatever they may do in original designs, should follow the mechanical details taught them by their foreign masters, and not devise indigenous methods of their own."

I need hardly say that there is not one word of truth in all this, and all that follows about "accomplished artists from Greece and Bactria" is merely a part of the hallucinations which disfigure his pages whenever he gets on the subject.

I have never ventured to state in words how long I fancy these massive wooden rails may have been in use before the time of Asoka; but my theory of the origin of Indian architecture necessitates an epoch of centuries at least. It must have required a very long time before so original a form could have been elaborated even in wood, with all its structural arrangements and all its adornments, both in architectural and figure sculpture, before we find it in the perfection it had attained in the age of Asoka. If I were asked to define my ideas more exactly, I should say four to five centuries, or before the advent of Buddha, and that their elaboration lasted as long afterwards, so that, if we put a thousand years for "the fifteen to thirty" of the Babu, it would represent the facts of the case and my meaning much more nearly. So far as our researches at present extend, Asoka was the first to copy in stone a form so familiar with his predecessors.[1] Luckily for us, for had he not, his rails, like all those that preceded, being in the more perishable material, might have disappeared like all the earlier ones. Whether he did so or not in consequence of a suggestion from the arts of a people using the more durable material, as above suggested, seems of very little consequence. The existence of the highly ornamented stone rails at Buddha Gaya (B.C. 250), and at Bharhut (B.C. 150), is in itself sufficient to prove that the Indians were far from undervaluing the use of that material for certain architectural purposes. If, in consequence, they refrained

[1] I do not feel quite sure that the Besnagar rail may not be older, but hardly much. ('Cunningham's Reports,' vol. x. plate xiii.).

from employing it in their architectural building, it was simply because they found—as the Burmese do at the present day—that wood was a better and more tractable material, and better suited in every respect for their purposes. The details of the Buddha Gaya rail are sufficient to prove that it was designed and erected by Asoka's own Indian workmen. No foreign influence was allowed to prevail except that perhaps of Persia, whose inhabitants were, for purposes of art at that time, practically the same people. The same is true of the Bharhut rail (150 B.C.); at Sanchi (100 A.D.), in the gateways, we first begin to feel the influence of Classic art; and at Amravati (350 A.D.), it is unmistakably evident.

It is more difficult to ascertain when the Indians left off using wood as their principal material for architectural purposes. From the bas-reliefs of the Sanchi gateways, executed in the first century of the Christian era, we learn with certainty that though the city walls and the foundation of their houses were of brick or stone, the upper and all the habitable parts were in wood, and all, in fact, that can be called architecture, was in that material only. Though the information is scant, and far from distinct, this appears to have been the arrangement from the earliest times to which our knowledge extends.

In the other direction the paintings in the Ajunta Caves show that down at least to the seveth century the pillars in all the porticos and the constructive parts were still of wood; generally richly painted; and stone architecture was the rarest possible phenomenon. On the other hand, however, in earlier caves, say of the fourth and fifth centuries, we find pillars, of forms that could not be derived from wooden originals, but must have been elaborated from stone models, either as used in the rock, or in buildings constructed on the plains. The presumption, therefore, is that at that early age, certainly before the fifth century, the Indians were familiar with the use of stone for architectural purposes, but continued the use of wood as their favourite material for long afterwards. The probability, in fact, is that the white ants—as before remarked —had a great deal more influence in settling this question than any æsthetic motives, or than any extraneous influence derived from any foreign sources.

There is only one other paragraph in the work of Buddha Gaya which it may be expedient to direct attention to before concluding what I have to say on the controversy between Babu Rajendralala and myself on the subject of the introduction of stone architecture into India. It is too long to quote, and besides contains no fact of any interest to any one, and even no contradiction of any statement of mine that would throw any light on the subject, it is, however, well worthy of attention as a psychological study by any one interested in the intellectual status of the Hindus, and is a curious example of that sort of mosaic, from different and frequently irrelevant documents, by which clever native vakils in Mofussil courts try to puzzle and obfuscate the slower intellects of Anglo-Saxon judges who generally preside.

It begins (p. 164) with a quotation from my 'History of Indian Architecture,' to every syllable of which I still adhere, and have not seen cause since to modify it in any way. It then goes on to a long extract from my book on 'Tree and Serpent Worship,' and winds up with a second quotation from the 'Architecture,' to which a wrong reference is given (query purposely?) The whole object of this long series of quotations being to convict me out of my own mouth of the crime of which the Babu first accused me in the 'Journal of the Asiatic Society of Bengal,' of maligning the most ingenious people of the world, by suggesting that they took a hint from foreigners on the use of stone for architectural purposes, and so his consistency and infallibility is proved and established. Any one, however, who has all my books before him—who has? and who will take the pains to study the paragraphs so run together, with the context—who will? will very soon see through this ingenious device. But even if any one is idle enough to make the attempt, he will not find it so easy. The reference to the 'Tree and Serpent Worship,' is to the first edition, and the reference to the last part of the quotation is avowedly wrong. When these difficulties are conquered, he will find the extracts from the 'Tree and Serpent Worship' are in a chapter which has no reference whatever to architecture, with which the beginning and end of the paragraph are concerned, but which is especially headed "Sculpture," and refers to that "Art" only. It was not consequently necessary to repeat that word every time that "the Art" to which the chapter was especially devoted and confined was mentioned. It was this omission, however, that enabled the Babu, by printing the extract from the 'Tree and Serpent Worship' between two paragraphs from architectural works, to make it appear that I had said that "Indian Architecture" "owes its origin to the influence of the Greek kingdom of Bactria"!

It is perhaps a unique instance of one author, in a controversy of this sort, trying to convict another of saying what there is not a shadow of proof he has ever said, and what the whole context of his works shows was as far as possible from his meaning. It is strange the Babu should persevere in such misrepresentations after the most distinct and positive denials on my part that I meant anything of the kind. It is possible that in my earlier works I did not state the negative side of the argument with the clearness I could now, but that was because it never occurred to me that any one could ever fancy that I meant to derive the architecture of India from Greek sources, all I have ever written and said on this subject being of exactly the opposite tendency. Its perfect originality is to me its keynote to its meaning and its especial charm.

It is one of the most curious and interesting facts that recent archæological researches have revealed to us, that there did exist in the north-west of India, especially beyond the Indus, a school of sculpture which undoubtedly owes its origin to the Greek colonists in Bactria, but whose period of greatest vigour was in the early centuries of the Christian era, long after the kingdom of Bactria had passed away. General Cunningham is of opinion that these sculptures belong to the most flourishing period of the Indo-Scythian rule under Kaniska and his immediate successors, or from B.C. 40 to 200 A.D.[1] He would, I

[1] 'Reports,' vol. v., Introduction, p. vi.

presume, be now inclined to bring their date somewhat lower; my own impression is that they extend to a very much more modern date.

The first person to give a detailed account of these, with the necessary illustrations, was Sir Edward Clive Bailey, in the twenty-first volume of the 'Journal of the Bengal Asiatic Society.' But, since then, many accounts have been published, and more than 1000 specimens have been accumulated in the Lahore Museum; nearly 200 in that at Calcutta. Dr. Leitner's collection, on loan, at South Kensington, and a considerable collection in the British Museum, enable European scholars to judge of their character, and besides these, there are many hundreds of specimens dispersed through private collections. All these, without one single exception, betray the influence of Classical art more or less distinctly; some—many indeed—so distinctly, that they would hardly be detected as foreign if placed in any museum of Byzantine or Mediæval art in Italy and other places in Europe. It has not yet been ascertained how much of this classical feeling is due to the influence of the original colony of Greeks left in Bactria by Alexander and his successors, or how much is due to subsequent international communication between the Byzantine Empire and the north-west of India; but, as the materials are now abundant, it is to be hoped that the investigation of this most important and interesting question will not be long delayed. Meanwhile what interests us most at this point, is that this school-art was confined wholly to the north-west of India. Its principal seat was in Gandara, beyond the Indus, and though it spread, sporadically, as far as Mathura, it nowhere can be traced beyond the Jumna, and was there met by a native school, having its origin apparently in Behar, but on which for a long time it had very little influence, and never entirely superseded.

Its architecture, so far as we know it, was almost exclusively of the Corinthian order. General Cunningham calls it the Indo-Corinthian style, but as such, it never penetrated into India, no specimens of it being found even as far as Mathura, so that it, more certainly than the sculptures, may be excluded from consideration in attempting to ascertain the origin of Indian architectural styles.

Is it that the Babu's eye is so uneducated, that he cannot perceive the obvious distinction between Classical and Native art in India? Or is it that he is so satisfied by his own superficial knowledge, that he has not cared to follow the recent developments of Indian archæology, and cannot consequently state them with intelligible clearness? The latter can hardly be pleaded as an explanation of the phenomena by the author of such volumes as we have been examining. Though the premisses are generally mistaken, and the conclusions drawn from them as generally erroneous, the mode of reasoning and the English in which it is expressed are wonderfully correct for a man writing in a foreign tongue, and dealing with a subject with which he had no previous acquaintance. Given the data, and assuming the conclusion, the logic is irreproachable, though the result is, notwithstanding, feeble and foolish.

The true explanation of the case I believe to be, that the curious mosaic in the work on Buddha Gaya is only an attempt to throw dust in the eyes of the public, and make it appear that he has proved his case. Not that the Greeks did or did not influence Indian art. This part of the case could easily have been stated in a few words, and proved or disproved in fewer still. With that point the Babu does not concern himself. But having in the article in the 'Bengal Journal,' in 1871, dressed up a gigantic bogie and labelled it with my name, he set himself vigorously to slay this being of his own creation, and all that he has written since has tended to the same desirable end, and thus to assure others of his triumph and his consistency. When he first set up this bogie, he knew perfectly well and knows now, that it was not the least like me, or any of my works; but having embarked in a wild crusade, and the Government having afforded him the means of maintaining it, as much nonsense has been written about it as was probably ever written about so absurd a controversy. The Government are too impersonal to feel how ridiculous they have rendered themselves by the part they have taken in the quarrel. The Babu has slain his bogie, much to his own satisfaction, and I don't feel a bit the worse. It will therefore be well if this absurd controversy is allowed to rest where it is, and the study of Indian archæology permitted to resume its practical course of scientific usefulness, undisturbed by any of those angry personal feelings which the Babu was the first, and I hope may be last, to introduce into a hitherto fascinating pursuit.

BRINDABUN.

To a person like myself, who from my boyhood has been drawing plans, and during my whole lifetime has been studying them, nothing appears more curious than the inability of even educated people to realise their form and appreciate their value. To me a plan of a building is in most cases more important for a correct understanding of its peculiarities than an elevation, or even a photograph of it, can be. To others it conveys very little information; and not only do they not see its connection with the superstructure, but they cannot judge how far it can be a necessary part of a building, even when other drawings are added showing the elevation of other parts.

That an uneducated man like Babu Rajendralala—I mean uneducated in the sense of plan-drawing, or architectural drawing of any sort—should blunder in this respect, is not perhaps to be wondered at. But when we find an educated English gentleman like Mr. Growse, a Master of Arts of Oxford, and who has strong building proclivities, failing entirely in this respect, it does become a wonder it is difficult to account for, and ought to make us tolerant of what seems a congenital deficiency. Certain it is, at all events, that throughout his work on 'Mathura'[1] his plans and drawings show a singular unlikeness to the buildings they are intended to represent, and that he also shows a curious insensibility to the fact, and a consequent intolerance of the works of others which present the opposite characteristics.

When I visited Brindabun in 1839, I was so much struck with the beauty, and at the same time with the interesting

[1] 'Mathura, a District Memoir.' By F. S. Growse, M.A., Oxon. Quarto, 1880. Government Press, North Western Provinces.

singularity, of the temple of Gobind Deo, that I spent some considerable time in examining it. I made a careful plan of it —as far as it was accessible to me—and a drawing of the interior. The latter I intended to have published in my 'Picturesque Illustrations of Ancient Architecture:' and would have done so had I been able to continue that publication; but want of encouragement prevented its going beyond the first four parts. The plan was published in 1867 in my 'History of Architecture,' with two views of the exterior of the building from photographs, woodcuts 260, 261 and 262. The plan was, like all those in that work, reduced to the scale of 100 feet to 1 inch, which was too small to do it justice; but in the present instance may be useful in correcting Mr. Growse's magniloquent comparison of it with St. Paul's Cathedral. By comparing it with my plan of the same church to the same scale, it will be perceived that it more nearly resembles one of the two small chapels, which are mere adjuncts to the western façade. But this is of little consequence; size is not its merit, and does not pretend to be. In beauty of outline and elegance of detail it is almost unrivalled, of its class, in India.

When I was making my survey, I was prevented from entering the sacrarium or cella. This I perfectly understood, and did not object to; but I was allowed to look through the bars of the doorway, and I could see dimly in the half light the images on their śinhasana; but what I did object to was, that I was not allowed by the attendant priests to approach, much less to measure, the west end of the building, on the outside. I consequently, in publishing the plan, indicated what I presumed was the form of this part, in outline only.

Fortunately for the vindication of my plan against Mr. Growse's strictures, Lieutenant (now Major) Cole, R.E., visited Brindabun in 1869, and in 1873 published a work in quarto on the antiquities of the place.[1] In this there is a plan of this temple of Gobind Deo on a considerably larger scale than mine, but confirming its exactness in every particular.

[1] 'Buildings near Muttra and Agra.' Photographs, plans, and drawings, by H. H. Cole, R.E., published by order of Government of India. India Office, 1873. Quarto.

As Major Cole is himself an accomplished plan-drawer, and was accompanied by a staff of competent surveyors, the plan, as far as it goes, leaves nothing to be desired. Like me, however, he was prevented by the priests from examining and measuring the western end of the building, and, like me, was obliged to be contented by sketching in, that part of the temple in outline, from what he could guess of its appearance, seen from a distance. After this, in 1880, Mr. Growse published his plan (p. 228), which is manifestly wrong on the face of it. In the first place, the dome does not fit the building, and, as he draws it, necessitates the contraction of the transepts to 18 feet internally; while they are, as seen at a glance, of the same width as the nave, 23 feet 6 inches, and the walls are throughout represented as solid, instead of being open colonnades of great beauty. The greatest defect of his plan, however, is, that it is impossible from it to understand how the west end is arranged. As he had free and unlimited access to this part of the building, if he had been able to draw a plan he could easily have solved the problem that Major Cole and I were prevented from doing, but as it is, he has left it more mysterious than before. That his representation of it is wrong, it is easy to see, but what the original arrangements were must remain a mystery till some one who can draw is allowed access to that part. In the meanwhile it is quite certain that the apartment which Mr. Growse calls the jagmohan is used as the sacrarium of the temple, and has been so used ever since the time of its erection. Whether it was intended to erect a second sacrarium beyond, I cannot of course say, not having seen the locality, and he would be a bold man who would predicate anything with certainty about buildings in so abnormal a style as that which prevailed in Brindabun during the tolerant reign of Akbar. But I entirely disbelieve the story of its having once existed, and being entirely razed to the ground by the Muhammadans. All these stories of Moslem bigotry appear to me to be singularly apocryphal, like those invented by Babu Rajendra to account for the inferiority of the architecture of the temple at Puri (*ante*, p. 62). When the Muhammadans wished to convert a temple into a mosque, or wanted materials to erect one, they never hesitated in destroying pagan temples for that purpose, but they never, so far as I know, gratuitously pulled down any of those buildings merely to gratify their feelings of religious intolerance. It was too tedious and expensive a process, while killing a cow in the precincts, and defiling the temple with its blood, could sufficiently desecrate it to render it useless at much less expense or trouble.

The other plans of temples published by Mr. Growse are nearly as bad as this one of Gobind Deo, but do not interest us so much. It is quite inconceivable, however, that any one could publish such a plan as that of the temple of Radha Ballabh, and publish next to it a view of the temple from a photograph,[1] and not to see that the one has no connection with the other, and does not in any way represent it; but throughout his work there runs the same inability to perceive this necessary connection between two illustrations of the same thing.

It would have been a fortunate circumstance for the buildings at Brindabun had Mr. Growse's architectural proclivities been confined to misrepresenting them in plans, but being the civilian in charge of the district, he had the command of funds he could apply to their restoration. It is fortunate that these were not equal to those at the disposal of Mr. Beglar, and that the buildings were of less importance, but their application was nearly as disastrous to the buildings operated upon. Mr. Growse first began his operations on the temple of Gobind Deo by removing a wall which gave height and picturesqueness to its outline, under the strange idea that it was built by the Muhammadans, and that his *bête noir*, Arungzebe, had used it as a mosque towards which to pray. A very little knowledge or thought would have shown him that as this wall ran east and west, no Muhammadan could use it for that purpose. Arungzebe did not worship the north polar star, and would not consequently turn to it in prayer. It was, in fact, a part of the original construction; the stone scaffolding or coring of the dome which it was intended to erect over the intersection of the nave and

[1] 'Journal, Asiatic Society of Bengal,' vol. xlvii. p. 1878, plates xii. and xiii.

transepts. By its removal, with that of all the accompanying construction, before any scientific examination was made, he has destroyed all chance of our ever being able to ascertain what was originally intended. I do not of course know, because I have never seen, but I feel perfectly convinced that any scientific architect could, from the springings, have been able to find out what was intended, but that chance is lost by Mr. Growse's restorations, which reduce the whole to one flat unmeaning outline (plate, page 224).[1] By this he may have mechanically preserved it from further decay, but this could easily have been done without interfering with its picturesqueness, or without attempting a restoration.

I have no photograph to show how far he was allowed to proceed with the erection of the sikhara over the present sacrarium, and there is none in his work to show its present state. He was, however, bent on completing it, and published in the forty-seventh volume of the 'Bengal Journal,' pl. xii., an elevation of what he conceived it ought to be. It is more like a representation of a cut-glass Birmingham pickle-bottle than anything any Hindu ever designed for any purpose, and if he had been allowed to carry out his design, he would have completed the destruction of this most beautiful temple. It is true it is difficult to say what was originally intended. Major Cole has sent me a tracing of the fresco at Amber, which is said in the inscription upon it, to be a representation of this temple, as it was intended to be finished. From its representation of the parts that are now standing, it is shown to be as incorrect as Hindu drawings of buildings generally are. Like our early mediæval artists, they represent buildings not as they are, but as they think they ought to be, and it requires both ingenuity and faith to recognise the resemblance.

If any attempt is ever made to restore it—which heaven forbid!—the design must be sought for among the temples of Brindabun itself. Nowhere else in India has a Muhammadan style been applied to Hindu temples in the same manner, and all experience derived from examples of Hindu architecture

[1] The plates in Mr. Growse's work not being numbered, there is great difficulty in referring to them correctly.

elsewhere, is quite inapplicable to this temple. We know it was not like what Mr. Growse proposed, but that is about the limit of our knowledge—at present at least.

Another building which was fortunately rescued from destruction by Sir George Couper's removal of Mr. Growse to a district where his architectural proclivities could do no harm, is the Sati Burj at Mathura. It was left unfinished by its founder, in 1570, and at some time during the last century was completed by a solid dome, which was certainly not that which was originally intended, but is more like it in outline than that proposed by Mr. Growse. Opposite page 138 he publishes a view of it from a photograph, and in juxtaposition, an elevation, drawn by a native, as he would propose finishing it. He says "he bestowed no small amount of time and thought upon it" (page 139), but the drawing is by a native assistant. It is characterised by that curious want of perception of relative proportion of parts, which apparently no native can correct, and that conventional mode of representing cornices which no European draftsman would perpetrate. But the most curious thing is the termination that Mr. Growse's architect proposed to substitute for the present one, more than a third of the height of the tower itself, and, if square in plan, crushingly heavy. It is not easy, however, from the mode in which it is drawn, to guess what its section is intended to have been, but this at least is evident, that it is ugly and incongruous to the last degree, and would have rendered it instead of an ornament a deformity that would have disgraced the beautiful situation it now occupies. I should have thought it would have required only a very slight familiarity with the architecture of Akbar's buildings at Agra, Secundra and Futtehpur Sicri, to see what was originally intended. From the basement to where it leaves off, the design inevitably suggests an open twelve-pillared pavilion, surmounted by a dome, making a composition a little taller than the present termination, but not unlike it in outline, and being open like hundreds of its class in the neighbourhood, without the crushing effect a solid termination must inevitably have produced.

As he has been removed to a district where there there are

no buildings on which he can exercise his misdirected activity, these criticisms are now of comparatively little interest to any one, though they may serve as a warning and a protest against the present mania for restoring the ancient buildings of India. As for Mr. Growse himself, I hope he may in future be forced to rest on the laurels he has already earned, by the erection of the Catholic church at Mathura,[1] one of the ugliest buildings that has been as yet erected in India, even by a European builder—which is saying a good deal—and by having done all that he was allowed to do, to destroy the temple of Gobind Deo, which is one of the most beautiful of its class.

[1] 'Mathura,' &c. Photographs opposite pp. 150 and 510.

APPENDIX A.

EXTRACTS from the REPORT of H. H. LOCKE, Esq., Principal of the Government School of Art, to H. S. BEADON, Esq., Officiating Under-Secretary to the Government of Bengal.—(No. 805, dated Calcutta, the 20th of July, 1869.)

SIR,—In continuation of my No. 761 of the 21st of May, to your address, I have the honour to submit the following memorandum.

2. The complete out-turn of work consists of—

A.—132, casts comprising 119 separate subjects from the following temples :—

Bhobaneswar	11	subjects.
Bhuggobatti	15	"
Kedareshwar	3	"
Mukteswar	19	"
Rajrani	18*	"
Kopaleshwari	10	"
Sisereshwar	1	"
Parusrameshwar	12	"
Sarideol	28	"
Anonymous	2	"
Total ..	119	"

B.—13 sheets of drawings from the following temples :—

Mukteshwar	5	sheets.
Kopaleshwari	3	"
Bhobaneswar	2	"
Bhuggobutti	1	sheet.
Plans of various temples	1	"
Survey map of Bhobaneswar	1	"
	13	

* One of these is an entire minaret, 35 feet high, in 12 pieces.

C.—33 photographs (8 inches × 10 inches) as under-noted :—

Mukteswar	3 plates.
Bhobaneswar	6 „
Juggernath	7 „
Udyagiri	4 „
Kanarak	3 „
Vaital Deol	2 „
Annuta Bashudeb	1 plate.
Rajrani	1 „
Brameshwar	1 „
Bhaskareshwar	1 „
Vindu Sarobar	1 „
	30

3. Of the 119 casts, 59 were what are technically called "squeezes," *i.e.* casts taken from clay matrices. For these it has been necessary to make piece-moulds.

5. After very careful estimation I find that the cost of producing sets of the above will be as under :—

(*a*) *Casts.*—Rupees 825 for the full set of 119 subjects. Smaller sets, costing from Rupees 150 upwards, could be selected and furnished to any of the Local Governments, or other bodies, which might not be prepared to expend the sum required for a full set. The cost of the different subjects of course varies considerably. Some of the smallest and simplest can be cast and finished for Rupees 2, while the Rajrani minaret (35 feet high) would cost Rupees 100. The average cost per subject may be considered as being Rupees 7, and very interesting sets might be made, consisting of 20, 30, 40 or 50 subjects and upwards, commencing at Rupees 150 for the smallest set (20).

(*b*) *Photographs.*—Rupees 30 for the set of 30 prints, unmounted, or Rupees 36, mounted on cardboard, with printed titles, &c. (the latter recommended).

(*c*) *Drawings.*—Until these are finished, I am unable to submit definite recommendations for their reproduction or estimates of cost. The casts and photographs are complete in themselves without the drawings, although the latter form, of course, a valuable supplement.

8. From the above statement it will be seen that the expenditure under every head, except that of "contingencies," has been kept

within the amount allowed by the Government of India. The item of "contingencies" exceeds the estimate by Rupees 787–3–1. It is of course in the very nature of a "contingency" to be less under one's control than any other item of expenditure, and in the present case many things have made it quite impossible for me to keep this item within the amount set down for it. I should, however, add that it includes some expenses which ought to be borne by the grant made to Baboo Rajendralala Mitra, and which, if so debited, would reduce the item as it now appears in my accounts to something nearer its estimated amount; but it is my intention to make this the subject of a separate communication to you.

APPENDIX B.

In the text of this work (p. 77) I have expressed myself strongly against Mr. Carlleyle and General Cunningham's determination of the site of Kapilawastu, without, however, having sufficient local knowledge to prove my case by fixing it myself. I am consequently anxious to justify my criticism, by pointing to a neighbouring and nearly as important site, regarding which I believe the General's views to be equally erroneous, and regarding which my local knowledge is nearly equal to his. It is with regard to the position of Saketa or Sha-chi, which he believes is identical with the old Hindu city at Ajudhya, or the modern Fyzabad, I, on the contrary, believe to be identical with Vaisaka or the modern Lucknow.

The leading authority on this subject is Fa Hian,[2] who describes the journey from Sankissa to Sravasti in considerable detail, and with approximate correctness as to distances, though, it must be confessed, these are not generally to be depended upon in his travels, unless otherwise confirmed. He relates his journey in the following terms:—

Sankissa to Canouge	7	yodjanas	S.E.	or 49	miles,	on map	52
Canouge to Holi	3	do.	S.	„ 21	„	„	21?
Holi to Sha-chi	10	do.	S.E.	„ 70	„	„	57
Sha-chi to Sravasti	8[3]	do.	N.E.?„	56	„	„	78
	28			196			208

[1] 'Cunningham's Reports,' vol. i. p. 317. 'Ancient Geography of India,' p. 401.

[2] Fa Hian. Beal's translation, p. 70.

[3] In Beal's translation of Fa Hian (p. 73), it is stated that there is avowedly an error in the Chinese text. It is there said that his direction from Sha-chi to Sravasti was "southwards," while it is evident, from the context, that it must have been in the opposite direction. Once the error is admitted, the correction may be whichever is most probable, either northwards or north-eastward.

In this narrative it is only necessary to remark, that Sha-chi, whether it is Saketa or Vaisaka, is the town where Buddha planted his toothbrush, which grew into a tree, which both he and Hiouen Thsang saw, and which, for the present at least, it will be convenient to call "Toothbrush Town." As both the travellers mention this object as a distinguishing feature of the locality, whatever its name may have been, there is consequently no doubt of their describing the same place.

The next authority is a party of pilgrims from Ceylon, mentioned by Spence Hardy in his 'Manual of Buddhism,' p. 334, who made the same journey from Sankissa to Sravasti, and make the distance 30 yodjanas, which is as nearly as may be the same distance as given by Fa Hian; it is consequently evident they followed the same route that he did. The direct distance as the crow flies is only 182 miles 26 yod. The pilgrim road was evidently through Sha-chi, which, though somewhat longer, may have presented more attraction and better accommodation than any direct route. General Cunningham says it is quite clear that Fa Hian's statement is erroneous, "because his distance would place Sha-chi in the neighbourhood of Lucknow." Why not? To avoid this, he is forced to extend Fa Hian's 10 yodjanas to 20, in order to reach Ajudhya, for which, of course, there is no authority. This may be necessary, but is hardly justifiable, unless it could be shown that Fa Hian was going to Ajudhya instead of turning northwards from Lucknow. But it entirely throws both his route and that of the Ceylonese pilgrims out of gear. They were not going to Ajudhya, but to Sravasti, and if by any mistake they had gone to Fyzabad, they must have added 7 yodjanas, or 49 miles to their 30, and travelled due north to reach their destination. This, it may be safely said, they did not do. In going from Sankissa to Sravasti, it would have been going very much out of their way to go to Ajudhya, where they had no business, yet it is the overlooking this fact which has apparently led the General astray in his determination of their route.

The great test of all this, however, is Hiouen Thsang's route, which extends from south to north, and consequently crosses Fa Hian's, stretching from east to west, both meeting in the "toothbrush town," about the middle of the route. There ought, consequently, be no difficulty in reconciling them, unless there is some great discrepancy in their measurements; but

[1] 'Ancient Geography,' p. 402.

in reality there is none, except those unnecessarily introduced by the supposed necessity of Ajudhya being one of the towns visited.

Hiouen Thsang starts from Kosambi, the position of which has been perfectly well ascertained by General Cunningham to be 32 miles west of Pryaga or Allahabad, on the Jumna. The distances from Kosambi to Fyzabad or to Lucknow are so nearly the same, that no indications of the route is to be obtained from this source. It is only by a careful study of the direction that it can be ascertained whether he visited the one city or the other. From Kosambi it is said: "Après avoir fait environ sept cents li (116 miles) dans une vaste forêt qui était située au nord-est de la caverne du dragon, il passa le Gange, et se dirigeant *au Nord* il arriva à la ville de Kâçapoura."[1] The cavern of the dragon alluded to in the above paragraph was situated, according to our author, 8 or 9 li, or a mile and a half to the south-west of the town, and in the forest, which extended over the south-eastern portion of the Doab. It is, however, apparently the description of the forest, which General Cunningham has mistaken for a description of the route which the text by no means bears out. The only words that apply directly to the route is "au nord," in order to reach Kasapura; which was thus, according to our author, situated due north of Kosambi, but has not yet been identified. From Kasapura the route was due north for 170 to 180 li (24 to 30 miles) to Visakha, or the "toothbrush" town. From this it appears to me impossible to assume that the pilgrim pursued a north-east route to Kasapura, and then a northern route to Ajudhya. He states, what is very probable, that in his time a vast forest extended from 7 or 8 li to the south-west of the town, over the whole of the lower Doab; but his route, whether through it or beyond the Ganges, was northward throughout. That this was so is proved beyond a doubt, it appears to me, by the next journey he made. "En partant de ce royaume, il fit environ 500 li (83 miles) au nord-est, et arriva au royaume de Çravasti." Measured on the map, Sravasti is as nearly as may be 80 miles to the north-east of Lucknow, while it is only 50 miles due north from Fyzabad. Either it is, therefore, that we must alter or reject the three authorities we have, bearing on the subject, or must accept their unanimous testimony that Sha-chi, Vaisaki, and Lucknow, were the same place, and that the celebrated tree that grew out of Buddha's tooth must have

[1] 'Si-yu-ki,' vol. i. p. 287.

been situated in the Constantia Gardens, or in some neighbouring locality where its descendants may possibly exist in the present day![1]

In the 'Hoei Li' (p. 122) there is an assertion that must be put down as an error, as it contradicts the 'Si-yu-ki,' always the better authority, and agrees with nothing. Leaving Kosambi, it is said—"De là il fit cinq cent li, *à l'est*, et arriva au royaume de Vaisaka"—500 li would take us neither to Fyzabad nor Lucknow, and the direction east would take him nowhere. He, however, describes Vaisaka as the "toothbrush town," and states that it is situated 500 li (83 miles) to the south-west of Sravasti, in exact accordance with the 'Si-yu-ki,' which fixes its position, and its identity with Lucknow, in so far as I can see, beyond doubt.

There is still another route recorded in the 'Hoei Li,'[2] which, though not bearing directly on the point at issue, throws considerable indirect light on the whole question. After residence three months at Canouge, on the banks of the Ganges, Hiouen Thsang determined to proceed, principally by water, to Pryaga or Allahabad. The distance between these two places is perfectly well known, being about 170 miles as the crow flies; but, strange to say, he has exaggerated all the distances, to an extent most unusual with him. Something may, of course, be due to the windings of the river, and something may also be owing to the difficulty of measuring the distances in a boat, but the discrepancies seem more than could arise from these causes. Together, they amount to 1700 li, or at the usual divisor to 283 miles. By the river the distance may be taken as about 200 miles, and the excess 83 miles, and may have been less in former times, and may probably be easy of adjustment from indications on the shore, which, however, has never been examined with reference to this, and we must in consequence leave it to future explorers. The first journey was made on the right bank of the river, 700 li, or 113 miles, where he crossed the river, into the kingdom of Ajudhya, in order

[1] I object, *in limine*, to any alteration in the text of an author, unless good reasons, independent of the facts stated, can be adduced for so doing. But in the present instance I would like to point out,—though without insisting upon it,—that, by adding a couple of yodyanas to Fa Hian's distance from Sachi to Sravasti—no great concession to so inaccurate a geographer—this route becomes identical with that of the Ceylonese pilgrims, and accords with that of Hiouen Thsang and with the maps in a most satisfactory manner. It being assumed, of course, that Lucknow was the toothbrush town, and not Fyzabad.

[2] 'Hoei Li,' p. 114.

to visit the sacred spots in the capital, presumably of the same name. There can be no mistake about its being on the banks of the Ganges, because he visited a great convent 4 or 5 li to the north-west—"de la capitale, près des bords du Gange." And as he had just left the Ganges at Canouge, and embarked at this city, whatever its name may have been, in a boat, to descend to Allahabad, he could not be mistaken as to the identity of the river. A little further on he mentions an ancient convent, about 40 li to the north, which he again describes as "Voisin du Gange;" so that there can be no inadvertence or mistake in the text. He must mean the river on whose banks he had been residing, and on which he was about to embark to proceed to Allahabad. The words of the 'Hoei Li' are—"il partit du royaume de Ayodhya, suivit le cours du Gange et avec 80 personnes qui s'étaient embarquées sur le même bateau," &c. (p. 116). If he had embarked on the Ghaghra, he certainly would have been a very long time in reaching Allahabad, as that river joins the Ganges a little above Patna, nearly 200 miles lower down the stream, which he would have been obliged to reascend in order to reach his destination. From the whole context it is evident that neither he nor any Buddhist pilgrim in those days visited the old capital on the Ghaghra. It never apparently was visited by Sakya Muni, and was not in consequence a sacred city of the Buddhist, though it was of the earlier Hindus.

Except a stupa, 200 feet high, and some convents, there do not appear to have been any very remarkable buildings in the city, and as the river here is constantly changing its bed, the probability is that there remains nothing now by which the site can be identified. The only fair inference, it seems to me, that can be drawn from this, is that in Hiouen Thsang's time, and for probably long before, the old Hindu capital of Dasaratha, on the banks of the Ghaghra, had been deserted and forgotten, and that a new capital for the kingdom of Ajudhya had been established on the banks of the Ganges: and the probability is, that this happened before Buddha's time, for, so far as I can make out, there is no Buddhist monument at Fyzabad, and no Buddhist tradition attaches to the spot.[1]

[1] Hiouen Thsang states (vol. ii. page 267) that the circuit of the kingdom of Ayodhya was 5000 li, or 833 miles, which General Cunningham (p. 385) has "no hesitation in rejecting as utterly beyond all possibility." To me it is only another proof that the Ayodhya on the Ganges, was only a substitute for the old capital in the Ghaghra of that celebrated kingdom.

All the traditions mentioned by Cunningham (404) of Buddhas residence for 9 or 19 years in the Jetavana monastery at Sravasti, and 6 or 16 at Sakepatura, would apply equally, or better, to Lucknow than to Fyzabad. So too would the legend of the noble maiden Vaisaka.

There is in fact nothing that Cunningham urges that would not apply to the one locality as well as to the other, except some modern definitions and determinations which appear to me extremely hazy, and no reliance can be placed on them either for or against either site.

Against this it may be argued that there are no signs of Lucknow being an old city, and no Buddhist remains have been found within its precincts. But have they been looked for? The same might have been said of Mathura twenty or thirty years ago, but now it has been found to be one of the most prolific sites for Buddhist remains in the north of India, and I see no reason for doubting that if the numerous maths or mounds which exist in Lucknow were excavated, they might yield a rich harvest; but if people make up their minds that it is only a modern city of the Nawabs of Oude, nothing will be attempted, and nothing found.

One of my main objects in writing this Appendix is to direct attention to what I believe to be the undoubted antiquity of the city, in hopes some one will open his eyes, and see if there may not be something worth looking at within its walls, or in its neighbourhood. If I am not very much mistaken in my reading of the authorities, as above set out, it is certain that Lucknow, and not Fyzabad, is the city in which Buddha resided for six years, and where he planted his toothbrush, which afterwards became the tree so famous in Buddhist legends, and is consequently where explorations could be carried out with the greatest probability of success for the elucidation of the history of the founder of the faith.